NEWS/400 TECHNICAL REFERENCE SERIES

Bryan Meyers
series editor

Desktop Guide to
RPG /400

by Julian Monypenny
& Roger Pence

Library of Congress Cataloging-in-Publication Data

Pence, Roger, 1953-
   Desktop guide to RPG/400 / by Roger Pence & Julian Monypenny
     p. cm. — (News 3X/400 technical reference series)
   Includes bibliographical references.
   ISBN 1-882419-18-9 (alk. paper). — ISBN 1-882419-11-1 (Series)
   1. RPG/400 (Computer program language) I. Monypenny, Julian, 1955- .
  II. Title. III. Series.
  QA76.73.R26P46 1996
  005.2'45—dc20   96-5169
                                                   CIP

Copyright © 1996 by DUKE PRESS
DUKE COMMUNICATIONS INTERNATIONAL
Loveland, Colorado

This book was printed and bound in the United States of America.

ISBN 1-882419-18-9

ISBN 1-882419-11-1 (*NEWS/400* Technical Reference Series)

1 2 3 4 5 6 KP 9 8 7 6

To my grandmother, for the joy she spreads around.
— J.M.

For my grandparents, who taught me that you can do anything if you try.
— R.P.

Acknowledgments

We'd like to thank Bryan Meyers for his thorough and very helpful job of tech editing this book (and for the routine or two of his we included); Erik Hymel for the code and testing he contributed; Katie Tipton for her hard work on the reference material; Mel Beckman and Paul Conte for always inspiring us to do better; Sharon Hamm for her dedication, hard work, and ability to endure any excuse; and Dave Bernard for his never-ending (it surely seemed) belief that we could really write this book. Roger would also like to thank FG, whose encouragement and support is very much appreciated. Julian would also like to thank Janie for her patience while he "burned the candle" working on this book.

Table of Contents

List of Figures

Chapter 9: Multidimensional Arrays

Chapter 10: Dynamically Determining Keypresses

Chapter 11: Getting and Setting the Cursor Position

Chapter 12: Using Named Indicators with Interactive Programs

Chapter 13: Using a Message Subfile to Display Error Messages

Chapter 14: Using Data Structures as Program Parameters

Chapter 15: Ending Interactive Programs Automatically

Chapter 16: Basic String Operations

Chapter 27: Using List APIs

Appendix B: String Functions Test Program

Appendix C: RPG Reference

Introduction

Chapter 1

Using This Book

If you are like many programmers, RPG is your bread-and-butter language. We'd like you to think of this book as your strawberry jam.

Ask any RPG programmer how many programs (s)he ever started from scratch and the answer will universally be, "None." Everybody "borrows" code: code skeletons, /COPY modules, and even old programs, to launch themselves into a new project.

We wrote this book to make it easy for you to borrow code. This book contains RPG snippets, routines, subroutines, /COPY modules, and even a little evangelical advice that you can use to write better, faster, and more reliable RPG. Included among the useful offerings here are string-handling routines, error-handling routines, advice for coding API calls, and numeric editing routines.

We don't spend a lot of time explaining concepts. For example, we include code to harness the power of file I/O feedback areas, but we don't explain those feedback areas. Rather, we assume you are at least conversationally familiar with file feedback areas. For any subject on which you think we moved too fast, check the *RPG User Guide* (SC09-1348) and the *RPG Reference Manual* (SC09-1349) for more details about that subject.

If you are like many AS/400 programmers, RPG is your bread-and-butter language. We'd like you to think of this book as your strawberry jam.

Style Guidelines

This book doesn't provide complete RPG programs, so you may wonder why we worry at all about style guidelines. The answer is consistency, reliability, and readability. With this book, our goal is to provide you with a set of "plug-in" RPG routines for use in your programs with a minimum amount of trouble and naming conflicts. Here are the style guidelines we have used throughout the book:

- Because of RPG's naming limitations, each routine or /COPY member's field names start with a specified two-character prefix. During testing and development, this two-character prefix ensured that these field names never conflicted with our test code. Beware, though, that if these prefixes (which are clearly indicated for each routine or member) conflict with naming conventions in your shop, you'll need to change them before you use these routines. None of the routines are very long and those changes, if necessary, will be minimal.

- We make extensive use of /COPY routines. Some RPG programmers don't like doing this (for whatever reason), but for us, the value of a proven routine, which can be used over and over again, is worth whatever trade-off in inconvenience the /COPY method provides. However, if you don't like our /COPY method, simply use the include facility from SEU (or your editor of choice) to copy the member directly into your source code.

- Because the layout of this book limited us to a minimal RPG line width, we don't use right-hand margin comments in our RPG code. You will, though, find full-line comments where necessary.

- Each routine or member includes an abstract that shows what other module dependencies it includes; what field values it expects; what field values it returns; any special requirements the routine or member may have (such as assuming that an F-spec somewhere declared a file feedback I/O data structure name); and what side effects, if any, a routine or member may provide. This abstract also clearly shows the member name (if the code shown is in a member of its own) and the two-character prefix that member's fields use.

- Many of the routines and techniques in this book show example RPG snippets using the appropriate code. These snippets are often abridged samples, not complete programs. We use the colon character (:) in column nine in these snippets to indicate where production RPG code would normally be found.

Effective RPG Error Handling

Chapter 2

Use these modules to provide standard, flexible error handling in your RPG programs — and an advanced OS/400 API-like error-reporting mechanism.

In this chapter, we provide the foundation for basic RPG error handling. The modules included in this chapter provide the code needed for basic error reporting and for returning errors from OS/400 APIs and user-written programs. Also included is a module to access the program-status data structure (which provides exception/error-handling information available to your RPG program). Like many of the other modules in this book, these modules are provided as /COPY members.

The first member provided, ERRDS (Figure 2.1), offers the data structure OS/400 APIs use to report errors. The following example shows this module being used with the QUSDLTUS (Delete User Space) OS/400 API. To use this module, use /COPY to include it in your RPG program's I-specs and check the value of the ERRDLN field after calling the API. If the API returns anything but a zero in ERRDLN, an error occurred using the API.

```
       /COPY ERRDS
         :
         :
       C                        MOVEL'MYSPC'   USNAM     P
       C                        MOVEL'MYLIB'   USLIB     P
         *
       C                        CALL 'QUSDLTUS'
       C                        PARM           USQNAM
       C                        PARM           ERRDS
         *
       C        ERRDLN   IFNE 0
         :                  ...Error processing here
       C                        ENDIF
```

The PGMSDS module (Figure 2.2) provides the data structure needed to make the program status data structure available to your RPG programs. This data structure reports exception/error-handling information. The data in this structure includes the RPG program's name, the name of the library in which the program is located, the job name and number, and the number of parameters passed to the program.

To use this module, use /COPY to include it in your RPG program's I-specs. Examples of using PGMSDS are shown in the next section of this chapter and in the technique provided in Chapter 3.

Advanced Error Handling

Members ERRDS and PGMSDS are simply definitions of standard data structures and are very straightforward; however, the other two members in this chapter are more complex. These members provide two modules: RERDS (Figure 2.3), which is a duplicate of the ERRDS data structure (Figure 2.1) used to return user error information to the calling program; and RERSET, which is an error-handling subroutine that uses modules ERRDS and RERDS. By using the RERDS and RERSET modules, your own programs can implement a flexible, OS/400 API-like error-reporting mechanism. Like that error handling, the error handling provided by subroutine RERSET is optional. Thus, you can build robust error handling into your RPG programs and use it when necessary, but also disregard it when necessary (as might be the case when you call an RPG routine from CL). Subroutine RERSET provides its optional error-handling capabilities by using the PSPRMS field in the PGMSDS data structure. This structure tells RERSET how many parameters were received when the program was called.

To use RERSET error handling in your programs, use /COPY to include the PGMSDS, ERRDS, and RERDS modules in your RPG program's I-specs and use /COPY to include the RERSET module in the subroutine area of your RPG program's C-specs. The optional ERRDS parameter should always be coded at the end of the parameter list. Immediately after the program's parameter list, use the Z-ADD op-code to set the value of the ERRPRM field (which is declared in the RERSET subroutine) to the number of parameters the program normally expects (remember to change this value if you ever modify the program and change the number of parameters). The ERRPRM field will be used by the RERSET subroutine to determine whether the optional error-handling data structure was passed to the program — thus determining whether error-handling information should be passed back to the caller through this structure.

For example, the following first stub of an RPG program calls the second stub (program TEST), passing the error-handling structure. The calling program is then able to interrogate the value of the ERRDLN field to determine whether an error occurred.

```
    /COPY ERRDS
     *
    C                       CALL 'TEST'
    C                       PARM            PARM1
    C                       PARM            PARM2
    C                       PARM            ERRDS
      :
    C           ERRDLN      IFNE 0
     *                      ...Error processing here
    C                       ENDIF


    - - - - - - - - - - - - - - - - - - - - - - - - - - - -


    * Program TEST
    /COPY PGMSDS
    /COPY ERRDS
    /COPY RERDS
     *
    C           *ENTRY      PLIST
    C                       PARM            PARM1
    C                       PARM            PARM2
    C                       PARM            RERDS
     * Set ERRPRM which indicates number of parameters
     * the program expects — don't forget to do this!
    C                       Z-ADD3          ERRPRM
      :
      :
     * This program ends with a call to RERSET to attempt
     * to return any error information available.
    C                       EXSR RERSET
    C                       MOVE *ON        *INLR
    C                       RETRN
     *
    /COPY RERSET
```

Let's also assume that you might occasionally call RPG program TEST from a CL program. When calling TEST from a CL program, you can omit the ERRDS parameter (which contains binary fields that are difficult to use in CL):

```
CALL PGM( 'TEST' ) PARM( Parm1, Parm2 )
```

In this case, the contents of Parm1 or Parm2 would need to be used to determine whether an error occurred in program TEST.

The RERSET subroutine provides solutions to two error-handling problems. First, because the error parameter is optional, it may not have been passed to the program, Second, the length of the error data field, RERDTA, in the caller may be shorter than the declared length in RERDS; if RERSET updates all of RERDTA, the area of memory immediately following RERDTA in the caller will be corrupted.

RERSET solves the first problem by comparing the actual number of parameters passed to the program (contained in the PSPRMS field of the PGMSDS data structure) to the number of the optional error parameters in field ERRPRM, which is set in a program's mainline before calling RERSET (note in the code on page 5 that this value is set to three, which is the number of parameters this stub expects). Setting ERRPRM in the program is very important: By manually setting ERRPRM to the number of parameters a program expects, and then comparing this value to the number of parameters actually received (from the PSPRMS subfield in the PGMSDS data structure), you can determine whether it is safe to return the error structure. RERSET solves the second problem by using the RERDSZ field passed from the caller, which defines the size of the error data field. RERDSZ is used with the SUBST op-code to set RERDTA to the correct length (memory could be corrupted in the calling program without this step).

Figure 2.1 ERRDS RPG Member

```
... 1 ...+... 2 ...+... 3 ...+... 4 ...+... 5 ...+... 6 ...+... 7 ...+... 8

   *-------------------------------------------------------------
   * ERRDS - Error data structure returned by APIs
   *
   * Function:
   *   Defines the error data structure returned by OS/400 APIs (or
   *   any similar program).
   *
   * ERRDS  - err_API_DS:
   *   ERRDSZ - err_data_size
   *   ERRDLN - err_data_len
   *   ERRID  - err_ID
   *   ERR016 - err_filler_16
   *   ERRDTA - err_data
   *-------------------------------------------------------------
IERRDS      IDS
I I           256                    B  1   40ERRDSZ
I                                    B  5   80ERRDLN
I                                       9   15 ERRID
I                                      16   16 ERR016
I                                      17  272 ERRDTA
```

Figure 2.2 PGMSDS Program-Status Data Structure

```
... 1 ...+... 2 ...+... 3 ...+... 4 ...+... 5 ...+... 6 ...+... 7 ...+... 8

   *-------------------------------------------------------------
   * PGMSDS - Program status data structure
   *
   * Function:
   *   Defines the Program Status data structure which is updated
   *   during the execution of an RPG/400 program.
   *
   * PGMSDS - pgm_sts_DS:
   *   PSPGM  - pgm_sts_pgm
   *   PSSTS  - pgm_sts_sts
```

Figure 2.2 PGMSDS Program-Status Data Structure, continued

```
... 1 ...+... 2 ...+... 3 ...+... 4 ...+... 5 ...+... 6 ...+... 7 ...+... 8
```

```
     *    PSSTSP - pgm_sts_prev_sts
     *    PSSEQ  - pgm_sts_src_seq
     *    PSSR   - pgm_sts_subr
     *    PSPRMS - pgm_sts_parm_nbr
     *    PSTYP  - pgm_sts_msg_type
     *    PSNBR  - pgm_sts_msg_nbr
     *    PSMSID - psm_sts_msg_id
     *    PSMI   - pgm_sts_mch_inst
     *    PSARA  - pgm_sts_work_area
     *    PSLIB  - pgm_sts_pgm_lib
     *    PSDTA  - pgm_sts_msg_data
     *    PSID   - pgm_sts_msg_id
     *    PSRS1  - pgm_sts_filler1
     *    PSFIL  - pgm_sts_file
     *    PSFILS - pgm_sts_file_sts
     *    PSJOB  - pgm_sts_job
     *    PSUSR  - pgm_sts_user
     *    PSJOBN - pgm_sts_job_nbr
     *    PSJOBD - pgm_sts_job_date
     *    PSPGMD - pgm_sts_pgm_date
     *    PSPGMT - pgm_sts_pgm_time
     *    PSCMPD - pgm_sts_compile_date
     *    PSCMPT - pgm_sts_compile_time
     *    PSCMPL - pgm_sts_compile_level
     *    PSSRCF - pgm_sts_src_file
     *    PSSRCL - pgm_sts_src_lib
     *    PSSRCM - pgm_sts_src_mbr
     *    PSRS2  - pgm_sts_filler2
     *-------------------------------------------------------------
IPGMSDS       SDS
I                                        1   10 PSPGM
I                                       11   15 PSSTS
I                                       16   20 PSSTSP
I                                       21   28 PSSEQ
I                                       29   36 PSSR
I                                       37  390PSPRMS
I                                       40   42 PSTYP
I                                       43   46 PSNBR
I                                       40   46 PSMSID
I                                       47   50 PSMI
I                                       51   80 PSARA
I                                       81   90 PSLIB
I                                       91  170 PSDTA
I                                      171  174 PSID
I                                      175  200 PSRS1
I                                      201  208 PSFIL
I                                      209  243 PSFILS
I                                      244  253 PSJOB
I                                      254  263 PSUSR
I                                      264 2690PSJOBN
I                                      270 2750PSJOBD
I                                      276 2810PSPGMD
```

Figure 2.2 PGMSDS Program-Status Data Structure, continued

```
... 1 ...+... 2 ...+... 3 ...+... 4 ...+... 5 ...+... 6 ...+... 7 ...+... 8

I                                       282 2870PSPGMT
I                                       288 293 PSCMPD
I                                       294 299 PSCMPT
I                                       300 303 PSCMPL
I                                       304 313 PSSRCF
I·                                      314 323 PSSRCL
I                                       324 333 PSSRCM
I                                       334 429 PSRS2
```

Figure 2.3 RERDS RPG Member

```
... 1 ...+... 2 ...+... 3 ...+... 4 ...+... 5 ...+... 6 ...+... 7 ...+... 8

*----------------------------------------------------------------
* RERDS - Return error data structure for user APIs
*
* Function:
*   Defines a copy of the Error data structure, ERRDS, returned
*   by OS/400 APIs, for error handling in user-written
*   programs or APIs.
*
* RERDS   - rtn_err_API_DS:
*   RERDSZ - rtn_err_data_size
*   RERDLN - rtn_err_data_len
*   RERID  - rtn_err_ID
*   RERO16 - rtn_err_filler_16
*   RERDTA - rtn_err_data
*----------------------------------------------------------------
IRERDS          DS
I                                       B   1    40RERDSZ
I                                       B   5    80RERDLN
I                                           9   15 RERID
I                                          16   16 RERO16
I                                          17 272 RERDTA
```

Figure 2.4 RERSET RPG Member

```
... 1 ...+... 2 ...+... 3 ...+... 4 ...+... 5 ...+... 6 ...+... 7 ...+... 8

*----------------------------------------------------------------
* RERSET - Set return error data structure
*
* Function:
*   Copies the API error data structure ERRDS to the data
*   structure RERDS for return to the calling program, if
*   RERDS was passed to the subprogram.
*
* Requires copy modules:
*   ERRDS   - Error data structure returned by APIs
*   PGMSDS - Program status data structure
```

Figure 2.4 RERSET RPG Member, continued

```
... 1 ...+... 2 ...+... 3 ...+... 4 ...+... 5 ...+... 6 ...+... 7 ...+... 8

 *    RERDS  - Return error data structure for user APIs
 *
 * Expects:
 *    ERRDS  - err_API_DS
 *    ERRPRM - err_parm_nbr
 *    PSPRMS - pgm_sts_parm_nbr
 *    RERDS  - rtn_err_API_DS
 *
 * Returns:
 *    RERDS  - rtn_err_API_DS
 *
 * Example:
 *    Return optional error parameter 5 to the caller.
 *
C*                    Z-ADD5         ERRPRM
 *                    ...
C*                    EXSR RERSET
C*                    RETRN
 *
 *----------------------------------------------------------------
C          RERSET    BEGSR
 *
C                    MOVE ERRPRM    ERRPRM  30
 *
 * Compare optional error parameter to number of parameters
 * passed to this program. If error passed, then return with
 * the length of data defined in the calling program
 *
C          PSPRMS    IFGE ERRPRM
 *
C                    Z-ADDERRDSZ    RERDSZ
C                    MOVELERRID     RERID
C                    MOVELERRO16    RERO16
C          RERDSZ    SUBSTERRDTA:1  RERDTA
 *
C          ERRDLN    IFLE RERDSZ
C                    Z-ADDERRDLN    RERDLN
C                    ELSE
C                    Z-ADDRERDSZ    RERDLN
C                    ENDIF
 *
C                    ENDIF
 *
C                    ENDSR
```

Gracefully Handling Unexpected Errors

Chapter 3

It's easy to write defensive RPG for errors you can anticpate, but you need this routine so your programs behave gracefully when unexpected errors occur and to make your RPG more robust and predictable.

The best defense against program errors is to predict and code for specific error possibilities in your RPG code. With careful planning and thought, you can write nearly bulletproof RPG programs without needing a generic error handler (i.e., code defensively against array index errors or attempts to divide by zero). However, there are times when an error occurs that you simply didn't anticpate. Your RPG should be robust enough to gracefully intercept these annoying errors and provide the investigative information you need to understand the cause and to help you avoid them in the future.

This chapter includes the code you need to provide your RPG with an effective and robust unexpected error handler to do just that. Together with RPG's program status data structure and RPG's program exception/error subroutine, *PSSR, this chapter's code will give you all the unexpected error protection you need (see Chapter 2 for more information about the program-status data structure). With this code in place, when an unexpected error occurs, the user is shown an informational screen with detailed error information; the system operator is notified that an error has occurred; a job log is printed; and a formatted RPG dump is performed. And after all that error reporting is completed, the offending RPG program ends.

To use this code in your programs, perform the following two tasks once:

- Create display file PSSRD with the DDS shown in Figure 3.1.
- Compile the CL program PSSRC with the code shown in Figure 3.2.

After creating these two objects, make sure they are available in a library in your AS/400's library list.Then, in any RPG program that you want to protect against unexpected errors:

- Include the /COPY statement for the CTLWDMP module (Figure 3.3) as the first line in your program (or, alternatively, ensure that column 15 of your program's Header specification has a 1 in column 15 — this entry is required to ensure a formatted RPG dump).

- Include the /COPY statement for the PGMSDS module (Figure 2.1 from Chapter 2) in the Input-spec area of your RPG program.

- Include the /COPY statement for the PSSR module (Figure 3.4) in the subroutine area of your RPG program.

For example, the following snippet of code will perform graceful error handling when divide-by-zero is attempted:

```
/COPY CTLWDMP
/COPY PGMSDS
*
C                       Z-ADDO        DIVISR  30
C               25      DIV  DIVISR    RESULT  30
C                       MOVE *ON       *INLR
*
/COPY PSSR
```

Figure 3.1 DDS Used by CL Program PSSRC

```
... 1 ...+... 2 ...+... 3 ...+... 4 ...+... 5 ...+... 6 ...+... 7 ...+... 8


*--------------------------------------------------------------------
* PSSRD - Display file for CL program PSSRD
*--------------------------------------------------------------------
A                                    DSPSIZ(24 80 *DS3)
A           R RECORD
A                             1 34'Program Error'
A                                    DSPATR(HI)
A                             3  2'This program has detected an error-
A                                  from which it cannot recover.'
A                                    COLOR(BLU)
A                             4  2'The System Operator has been notif-
A                                  ied.'
A                                    COLOR(BLU)
A                             5  2'Press Enter to cancel this program-
A                                  .'
A                                    COLOR(BLU)
A                             6  2'The Data Processing Department wil-
A                                  l contact you with instructions.'
A                                    COLOR(BLU)
A                             8  2'Job name . . . . :'
A           SDSJOB     10   0  8 23
A                             9  2'User profile . . :'
A           SDSUSR     10   0  9 23
A                            10  2'Job number . . . :'
A           SDSNBR      6   0 10 23
A                            12  2'Program  . . . . :'
```

Figure 3.1 DDS Used by CL Program PSSRC, continued

```
... 1 ...+... 2 ...+... 3 ...+... 4 ...+... 5 ...+... 6 ...+... 7 ...+... 8

A              SDSPGM       10  O 12 23
A                            13  2'Status code  . . :'
A              SDSSTS        5  O 13 23
A                            14  2'Statement number :'
A              SDSSEQ        7  O 14 23
A                            15  2'Error message  . :'
A              SDSERR        7  O 15 23
A                            16  2'Message text . . :'
A              SDSMSG       80  O 16 23
A                            23  2'Press Enter to continue.'
A                                COLOR(BLU)
```

Figure 3.2 CL Program to Convey Error to User

```
... 1 ...+... 2 ...+... 3 ...+... 4 ...+... 5 ...+... 6 ...+... 7 ...+... 8

/*
 | ------------------------------------------------------------ +
 | PSSRC CL program to post a message to a user and print     +
 | job log when a program ends abnormally.                    +
 | Called from *PSSR subroutine in member PSSR.               +
 | ------------------------------------------------------------ +
 */

PGM PARM( &SDSSTS                                              +
          &SDSPGM                                              +
          &SDSSEQ                                              +
          &SDSERR                                              +
          &SDSMSG                                              +
          &SDSJOB                                              +
          &SDSUSR                                              +
          &SDSNBR  )                                           +

DCL    &SDSSTS   *CHAR    5
DCL    &SDSPGM   *CHAR   10
DCL    &SDSSEQ   *CHAR    7
DCL    &SDSERR   *CHAR    7
DCL    &SDSMSG   *CHAR   80
DCL    &SDSJOB   *CHAR   10
DCL    &SDSUSR   *CHAR   10
DCL    &SDSNBR   *CHAR    6

DCLF       FILE( PSSRD )
SNDMSG     MSG( 'Job'   *BCAT  &SDSNBR *TCAT '/'    *TCAT  +
                &SDSUSR *TCAT   '/'     *TCAT &SDSJOB *BCAT +
                'has encountered an error with program'    +
                *BCAT   &SDSPGM         *TCAT              +
                '. Examine RPG dump and job log.' )        +
           TOUSR( *SYSOPR )                                 +
           MSGTYPE( *INQ )
SNDRCVF
```

Figure 3.2 CL Program to Convey Error to User, continued

```
... 1 ...+... 2 ...+... 3 ...+... 4 ...+... 5 ...+... 6 ...+... 7 ...+... 8

DSPJOBLOG  OUTPUT( *PRINT )

ENDPGM
```

Figure 3.3 RPG Control Spec with DEBUG On

```
... 1 ...+... 2 ...+... 3 ...+... 4 ...+... 5 ...+... 6 ...+... 7 ...+... 8

 *----------------------------------------------------------------
 * CTLWDMP - Program control spec with DUMP specified for a
 *           formatted RPG dump.
 *
 * This header specification is required by the *PSSR
 * subroutine in member PSSR to create a formatted RPG dump
 * when an abnormal program end occurs.
 *----------------------------------------------------------------
 *
H          1
```

Figure 3.4 PSSR Subroutine Module

```
... 1 ...+... 2 ...+... 3 ...+... 4 ...+... 5 ...+... 6 ...+... 7 ...+... 8

 *----------------------------------------------------------------
 * PSSR  - Program exception/error subroutine
 *
 * Requires copy modules:
 *   CTLWDMP  - Program header with a '1' in column 15
 *   PGMSDS   - Program status data structure
 *
 * Returns:
 *   Ends program and posts message to user and to job log.
 *----------------------------------------------------------------
C          *PSSR     BEGSR
C                    CALL 'PSSRC'                    99
C                    PARM          PSSTS
C                    PARM          PSPGM
C                    PARM          PSSEQ
C                    PARM          PSMSID
C                    PARM          PSDTA
C                    PARM          PSJOB
C                    PARM          PSUSR
C                    PARM          PSJOBN
C                    DUMP
C                    ENDSR'*CANCL'
```

Using the File Information Data Structure

Chapter 4

File information data structures provide your RPG programs with useful exception, error-handling, and hard-to-get runtime information about disk and printer files.

You can define a file information data structure (INFDS) for each file to make file exception/error information available to your RPG programs. Each file can have an associated file information data structure, but each file's structure must be unique to that file (i.e., an INFDS cannot be shared between two files).

Some of the information provided in a file's INFDS is useful for debugging or testing purposes. For example, a status code is available (positions 11-15) to indicate the status of the last file operation performed. In addition to debugging or testing, your program may need INFDS information for runtime application purposes. For example, the current print line (positions 367-368) is tracked for printer files (if you need to manually track overflow), and you can also use the INFDS to determine the record length of a disk file. In addition, an INFDS can tell you the name of a file as it is specified on the F-spec (in positions 1-8) and the actual name of the file, which would be different from the F-spec name if a file override is being used (in positions 83-92).

Member FINFDS (Figure 4.1) contains the RPG module required to "snap" in a file information data structure for a file. As you can see, lots of handy data is available in an INFDS. (In the next chapter, we'll provide an abbreviated INFDS for workstation files, which is handy for cursor management and subfile relative record number tracking.) Note that our INFDS member doesn't contain *all* the subfields available for a disk or printer file, but it does contain the most commonly used subfields. If you have a special use that requires subfields we haven't provided, simply add them to the FINFDS module. See the *RPG Reference Manual* (SC09-1817) and the *Data Management Guide* (SC41-3710) for detailed information about all the subfields available in the file information data structures.

To provide an INFDS for any file in your RPG programs:

- Include the /COPY statement for the FINFDS module in the I-spec area of your RPG program.
- For every file for which you need a file information data structure, code the "KINFDS" entry in positions 53-58 and the name of an associated file-specific data structure in positions 60-65 on that file's F-spec.
- In the I-spec area, code a data structure I-spec for each data stucture you named in the previous step. Make sure that the name specified in positions 7-12 matches the name supplied in the F-spec in columns 60-65. Also, be sure to code these file information data structures with a 512-byte length.

The sample code below shows a snippet of RPG that provides two file information data structures, one for a disk file and one for a printer file. After each file operation, you can move one of these data structures into the FINFDS data structure (specified in the FINFDS /COPY module) to make the data structure's subfields available to your RPG program. Note the technique here of specifying a data structure length of 512 on both the FINFDS data structure in the /COPY module and in each file-specific data structure you need. This makes it easy to move the contents of one data structure to another (i.e., it makes it easy to map the information in a 512-byte block of file-specific data to the subfields defined in FINFDS). With this technique, no subfields are needed in the file-specific data structures you provide.

```
FMYFILE  IF  E                     DISK          KINFDS MYIFDS
FQSYSPRT O   F     132             PRINTER       KINFDS QSIFDS
 *
 /COPY FINFDS
IMYIFDS     IDS                              512
IQSIFDS     IDS                              512
    :
    :
 * After a file operation to MYFILE, make its
 * file information data structure available.
C                         MOVELMYIFDS    FINFDS
 *
 * After a file operation to QSYSPRT, make its
 * file information data structure available
C                         MOVELQSIFDS    FINFDS
```

Figure 4.1. File Feedback Module INFDS for Disk and Printer Files

```
  ... 1 ...+... 2 ...+... 3 ...+... 4 ...+... 5 ...+... 6 ...+... 7 ...+... 8

 *---------------------------------------------------------------
 * FINFDS - File information feedback data structure
 *
 * Function:
 *   Defines disk and printer file feedback area.
 *
 *   FINFDS - file_inf_DS
 *     FIFPN     file_name (from program)
 *     FIOPN     file_open
 *     FIEOF     file_eof
 *     FISTS     file_sts
 *     FIOPCD    file_opcode
 *     FIRTNN    file_rpg_routine
 *     FISTN     file_src_nbr
 *     FIRCDN    file_rcd_name
 *     FIMGID    file_msg_id
 *     FIODP     file_odp
 *     FIFINA    file_name_actual
 *     FILINA    file_lib_name
 *     FISPNA    file_splf_name
 *     FISLNA    file_splf_lib
 *     FISPLN    file_splf_nbr
 *     FIRECL    file_recl
 *     FIMBRN    file_mbr_name
 *     FIFTYP    file_type
 *     FIROWS    file_rows
 *     FICOLS    file_cols
 *     FIRECS    file_recs_at_open
 *     FIATYP    file_access_type
 *     FIDUPK    file_dupe_key
 *     FISRCF    file_src_ind
 *     FIOFLN    file_of_line_nbr
 *     FIFMTN    file_last_format
 *     FIRLEN    file_recl_pro
 *     FILNNO    file_line_nbr
 *     FIPGCT    file_page_cnt
 *     FIKEYF    file_nbr_keys
 *     FIKEYL    file_key_len
 *     FIMBRN    file_mbr_nbr
 *     FIRRN     file_rrn
 *     FIKEYV    file_key_val
 *---------------------------------------------------------------
IFINFDS        DS                              512
I                                        1    8 FIFPN
I                                        9    9 FIOPN
I                                       10   10 FIEOF
I                                       11  150FISTS
I                                       16   21 FIOPCD
I                                       22   29 FIRTNN
I                                       30   37 FISTN
I                                       38   45 FIRCDN
```

Figure 4.1. File Feedback Module INFDS for Disk and Printer Files, continued

```
... 1 ...+... 2 ...+... 3 ...+... 4 ...+... 5 ...+... 6 ...+... 7 ...+... 8

I                                      46  52 FIMGID
I                                      81  82 FIODP
I                                      83  92 FIFINA
I                                      93 102 FILINA
I                                     103 112 FISPNA
I                                     113 122 FISLNA
I                                   B 123 1240FISPLN
I                                   B 125 1260FIRECL
I                                     129 138 FIMBRN
I                                   B 147 1480FIFTYP
I                                   B 152 1530FIROWS
I                                   B 154 1550FICOLS
I                                   B 156 1590FIRECS
I                                     160 161 FIATYP
I                                     162 162 FIDUPK
I                                     163 163 FISRCF
I                                     188 189 FIOFLN
I                                     261 270 FIFMTN
I                                   B 283 2860FIRLEN
I                                   B 367 3680FILNNO
I                                   B 369 3720FIPGCT
I                                   B 387 3880FIKEYF
I                                   B 393 3940FIKEYL
I                                   B 395 3960FIMBRN
I                                   B 397 4000FIRRN
I                                     401 499 FIKEYV
```

Declaring Data Types

Chapter 5

Make your code more bulletproof and easier to troubleshoot by declaring variables to be of standard "types."

Quick, what is the fatal error in the following RPG snippet?

```
C                             Z-ADD1         X        10
C           X                 DOWLE10
C                             .
C                             . Some code
C                             .
C                             ADD   1        X
C                             ENDDO
```

Something is very wrong here. Did you find the error? Here's a hint: How many times will the loop above be executed?

The code implies 10, doesn't it? But the correct answer isn't 10. This RPG code will cause an infinite loop, continually executing the code within the body of the loop. Why? Because the variable x has been declared as a one-digit variable. When x's value is nine, and one is added to it, its new value becomes, not 10 as desired, but rather zero! This error could have been avoided if x had been declared as a two-digit value — but then pity the poor maintenance programmer who three years later needs to change the loop to perform 100 times.

A solution to arbitrarily assigning data types and data lengths is to use standard data "types." Figure 5.1 shows the STDTYPES RPG member, which declares five data types: boolean, character, integer, long integer, and message ID. To use this member, simply copy it into your RPG program's I-specs with /COPY and then declare variables as needed with the DEFN operation code, as shown in the following example. In this example, X is declared as an integer, COUNT is declared as a long integer, CUSTYP is declared as a character, and MSGID is declared as a message ID. It's probably best to put the like defines in the *INSR subroutine.

```
I/COPY STDTYPES
    :
C            *LIKE      DEFN #INT    X
C            *LIKE      DEFN #LINT   COUNT
C            *LIKE      DEFN #CHAR   CUSTYP
C            *LIKE      DEFN #MSG    MSGID
```

Note that the integer data type, as defined in STDTYPES, provides an integer value with up to five digits. Thus, there is some possibility of overflowing even that value in a loop counter; but it isn't very likely. If you're not sure whether or not the five-digit integer type is long enough, use the long integer type.

Don't hard-code library or source file names on /COPY statements!

We normally place /COPY members in a source file named QRPGSRC in a copy book library. Putting this library in the library list makes the included members available without needing to hard-code the library and source file name in the /COPY statement. This makes it easy to change the name of the copy book library in the library list, and test or use different versions of the includes. The /COPY examples shown in this book never include library or source file names.

Figure 5.1 STDTYPES Standard Data Type Declarations

```
... 1 ...+... 2 ...+... 3 ...+... 4 ...+... 5 ...+... 6 ...+... 7 ...+... 8

 *--------------------------------------------------------------*-----------------
 * STDTYPES - Standard program data type declarations.
 *
 * Function:
 *    Defines standard data type templates.
 *
 *    #BOOL  - Boolean
 *    #CHAR  - Character
 *    #INT   - Integer
 *    #LINT  - Long integer
 *    #MSGID - Message id
 *--------------------------------------------------------------*-----------------
I            IDS
I                                          1    1 #BOOL
I                                          2    2 #CHAR
I                                          3   70#INT
I                                          8  220#LINT
I                                         23   29 #MSGID
```

Mapping Externally Described Fields to Array Elements

Chapter 6

Overcome an annoying constraint of RPG's externally described files with this field-to-array mapping technique.

RPG/400's externally described files offer many advantages over program-described files, especially in terms of ensuring reliability and consistency. There are, however, a few annoyances associated with externally described files. Specifically, you may find it challenging to effectively map fields in an externally described file to array elements. So in this chapter, we provide a technique that maps fields in an externally described record to an array. Our example shows that the fields being mapped are stored contiguously in the file, but the technique would also work for non-contiguous fields.

Consider the LEDGER file described by the DDS shown in Figure 6.1. This is a general ledger master file; its records contain summary information about general ledger accounts. Included in this information is a group of 12 contiguous fields (LECJAN through LECDEC) that represent monthly balances for an account.

In many RPG programs, it would be far handier to deal with these contiguous monthly balance fields as elements of an array rather than dealing with them directly by explicit field name. For example, consider summing monthly balances up to and including a given month (e.g., when you need to calculate the ending balance through May to print a May financial statement). Using an array, where the field ENDMON is the ending month number, the following four lines of code are all that you need to calculate any given month's ending balance:

```
C                          Z-ADDO          ENDBAL
C              1           DO     ENDMON    X
C              CUR,X       ADD    ENDBAL
C                          ENDDO
```

This coding would be far more complex if it were done by referencing the individual field names of each of the 12 monthly balances. Thus, the challenge is to effectively map the externally described fields to array elements.

You can use several techniques to map the field names to array element names, including using external data structures and hard-coding overlapping fields with program-described data structures. These methods, though, are error-prone because of their high sensitivity to field positions in the file. The most straightforward and easy-to-maintain method for mapping the field names to array element names is to simply use the RPG I-spec field-renaming facility to rename the externally described field names to array element names.

For example, the code below maps the 12 monthly balance fields in the LEDGER file to array elements of the CUR array:

```
FLEDGER   IP  E                       DISK
 *
E                          CUR        12  9 2
 *
ILEREC
I                 LECJAN                          CUR,1
I                 LECFEB                          CUR,2
I                 LECMAR                          CUR,3
I                 LECAPR                          CUR,4
I                 LECMAY                          CUR,5
I                 LECJUN                          CUR,6
I                 LECJUL                          CUR,7
I                 LECAUG                          CUR,8
I                 LECSEP                          CUR,9
I                 LECOCT                          CUR,10
I                 LECNOV                          CUR,11
I                 LECDEC                          CUR,12
```

RPG's I-spec renaming facility makes the original field name (e.g., LECJAN) unavailable to your RPG program. If you need to reference an array element value in DDS (for printer or display files), you'll need to assign fields to an RPG program for that purpose. For example, if your DDS uses the field name MBJAN to display the LECJAN field (which has now been mapped to the CUR,1 array element), simply insert Z-ADD CUR,1 to MBJAN before your program writes the display file format, as follows:

```
C                      Z-ADDCUR,1      MBJAN
```

This renaming method is superior to other field-to-array mapping techniques because it is less dependent on physical field positions to work — the code to rename the fields doesn't require a knowledge of field beginning or ending positions. The I-specs used to rename the fields are completely independent of field positions in the file. Be aware, though, that the array declaration is dependent on the file layout — if the LEDGER file were changed to make all 12 monthly balance fields 10 bytes long instead of 9 bytes long, the mapping would fail if the CUR array definition was not changed.

To simplify coding changes across many programs, consider creating external modules that declare the target array and that rename the LEDGER file fields (as shown in Figure 6.2 and Figure 6.3). By isolating this code in these modules, you would only have one place to maintain each definition should the layout of the LEDGER file ever change. Using these modules reduces the coding necessary to map the fields to array elements.

```
FLEDGER  IP  E                        DISK
 *
 /COPY GLARR
E... other E-specs as necessary
 *
I... other I-specs as necessary
I...
 /COPY LECARR
```

The GLARR member goes anywhere in the RPG program's E-Specs and the LECARR member goes anywhere in the RPG program's I-specs.

Figure 6.1. LEDGER File DDS

```
... 1 ...+... 2 ...+... 3 ...+... 4 ...+... 5 ...+... 6 ...+... 7 ...+... 8

A                                         UNIQUE
A         R LEREC
A           LESTOR        4S 0
A           LEACCT        4S 0
A           LEDEPT        1S 0
A           LELOC         2S 0
 *
A           LECODE        3A
A           LEDRCR        1A
A           LENAME       24A
 *
A           LECBEG        9P 2
 *
A           LECJAN        9P 2
A           LECFEB        9P 2
A           LECMAR        9P 2
A           LECAPR        9P 2
A           LECMAY        9P 2
A           LECJUN        9P 2
A           LECJUL        9P 2
A           LECAUG        9P 2
A           LECSEP        9P 2
A           LECOCT        9P 2
A           LECNOV        9P 2
A           LECDEC        9P 2
```

Figure 6.1. LEDGER File DDS, continued

```
... 1 ...+... 2 ...+... 3 ...+... 4 ...+... 5 ...+... 6 ...+... 7 ...+... 8

  *
A           K LESTOR
A           K LEACCT
A           K LEDEPT
A           K LELOC
```

Figure 6.2 Member LECARR, Which Maps LEDGER File Monthly Balances to Elements of the CUR Array

```
... 1 ...+... 2 ...+... 3 ...+... 4 ...+... 5 ...+... 6 ...+... 7 ...+... 8

  * Rename LEDGER file monthly balances to CUR array elements.
  * Requires that member
ILEREC
I           LECJAN                          CUR,1
I           LECFEB                          CUR,2
I           LECMAR                          CUR,3
I           LECAPR                          CUR,4
I           LECMAY                          CUR,5
I           LECJUN                          CUR,6
I           LECJUL                          CUR,7
I           LECAUG                          CUR,8
I           LECSEP                          CUR,9
I           LECOCT                          CUR,10
I           LECNOV                          CUR,11
I           LECDEC                          CUR,12
```

Figure 6.3 Member GLARR, Which Declares CUR Array to Hold LEDGER File Monthly Balances

```
... 1 ...+... 2 ...+... 3 ...+... 4 ...+... 5 ...+... 6 ...+... 7 ...+... 8

  * Twelve-element array to hold GL monthly balances
E                       CUR         12  9 2
```

Sorting Arrays

Chapter 7

Replace RPG's SORTA op-code with the templates in this chapter for a more flexible way to sort arrays.

It's a simple fact of life: The more you have, the more you want. RPG's sort array (SORTA) op-code is a typical example of this maxim. At first, the capability to sort a whole array in ascending order appears to satisfy every need. Then you start hitting the quirky programs: In one you need to sort the front end of an array, leaving the blank elements at the end; in another you need to sort an array in descending order. The two templates in this chapter provide different approaches to solving both these problems. You won't need these templates every day, but it's handy to know you have them in reserve for when the occasion arises.

In this chapter we use templates, not /COPY modules. A template is a generic member you copy into a source program using SEU and then modify to fit the program's specific requirements. We use templates because every array is unique. To manipulate an array, you must work with the actual array — you can't just copy it to an all-purpose array and then execute some generic function. The templates included in this chapter are

ARYSRT   provides a simple way to sort small arrays of up to approximately 200 elements (Figure 7.1).

ARYQSRT   provides a complex way to sort arrays of any size very quickly (Figure 7.2).

Both templates provide exactly the same functionality; the only difference is performance. The time required to run ARYSRT increases exponentially with the size of the array; whereas ARYQSRT exhibits the same performance characteristics as the SORTA op-code, with the sort time increasing logarithmically with the size of the array. Because both templates are very simple to incorporate into your programs, we recommend you use ARYQSRT. Although ARYQSRT contains more code, it only requires one additional substitution, making it almost as easy to "plug in" as ARYSRT is.

Let's look at a simple example of how to use the templates. Suppose you are writing a program to validate the class of an item. Because class validation occurs often in this program, and because the ITMCLS file is a known, relatively static size, it makes sense to store the item classes in an array for fast access:

```
*
* Item class file
FITMCLS  IF  E                    DISK
*
* Item class array
E                    CLS      200  4
*
* Size of item class array
I          200                C          CLSSIZ
*
* Load item class array
C                    Z-ADD0    C      50
C                    READ ITMCLS              99
C       *IN99        DOWEQ*OFF
C                    ADD  1    C
C                    MOVE ICCLS  CLS,C
C                    READ ITMCLS              99
C                    ENDDO
```

The CLSSIZ named constant defines the declared size of the CLS array. The C field is used as an index to the array, and after the DOWEQ loop, contains the actual number of elements in the array.

Then you add the code to sort the array using the ARYSRT template in three simple steps. First, you key the code to execute the sort function:

```
*
* Sort only filled elements of item class array.
C                    Z-ADD1    CLSBOT  50
C                    Z-ADDC    CLSTOP  50
C                    EXSR CLSSRT
```

where CLSBOT and CLSTOP define the actual bottom and top entries used in the array, and the subroutine name consists of the array name followed by SRT. When subroutine CLSSRT is executed, it only sorts the CLS array from the elements at CLSBOT to CLSTOP, leaving any blank elements beyond CLSTOP at the end of the array. If you want to include blank elements in the sort and move them to the front of the array, you set CLSTOP to the declared size of the array in CLSSIZ before executing CLSSRT, as shown below:

```
*
* Sort all elements of item class array.
C                    Z-ADD1    CLSBOT  50
C                    Z-ADDCLSSIZ  CLSTOP  50
C                    EXSR CLSSRT
```

Next, you copy the ARYSRT template (Figure 7.1) into the source program at the end of the C-specs. Finally, you execute the following change commands on the SEU command line to replace the generic values in the template with the specific values for the item class array:

```
C  &ar     CLS     A
C  &len    ' 4 '   A
C  &temp   CLSTMP  A
C  &bot    CLSBOT  A
C  &top    CLSTOP  A
```

&ar is replaced by the array name CLS, and creates a subroutine name of CLSSRT. Please note that the array name must be 3 characters long; otherwise, code can be shifted to the left or right, resulting in syntax errors. &len is replaced by both the length of an element and its number of decimal places, as used in columns 49 to 52 of a C-spec. &temp is replaced by the name of a work variable used to store an element from the array. &bot and &top are replaced by the CLSBOT and CLSTOP fields mentioned above.

To use the ARYQSRT template (Figure 7.2) instead of ARYSRT, you follow the steps described above and execute one additional change command on the SEU command line:

```
C  &pivot  CLSPVT  A
```

&pivot is replaced by the name of a work variable used to store an element from the array.

By default, both templates sort an array in ascending order. However, the sort templates include a boolean flag named ARYDSC which, when set to *ON, overrides the default behavior of the sort routines. To sort an array in descending order, you simply set field ARYDSC on before executing the sort subroutine:

```
 *
 * Sort item class array in descending order
C                      Z-ADD1      CLSBOT  50
C                      Z-ADDC      CLSTOP  50
C                      MOVE *ON    ARYDSC
C                      EXSR CLSSRT
```

The sort templates in this chapter show how you can improve upon the standard functionality in RPG/400. With the right algorithm, as shown by ARYQSRT, you can also achieve this without loss of performance. As well as being useful for sorting arrays, the templates can serve as blueprints for sorting other storage areas, such as multiple-occurrence data structures or user spaces. The next chapter shows how, in conjunction with these sort routines, you can code a speedy, more functional replacement for RPG's LOKUP operation code.

Figure 7.1 ARYSRT Sort Array Template

```
... 1 ...+... 2 ...+... 3 ...+... 4 ...+... 5 ...+... 6 ...+... 7 ...+... 8

    *-----------------------------------------------------------------
    * ARYSRT   Sort array template
    *
    * Function:
    *   Sorts an array between the specified bottom and top
    *   entries in either ascending or descending order.
    *
    * Usage:
    *   Copy this template into your program and replace all
    *   &values listed below with your actual program variables.
    *   Syntax errors will occur if the array name is not 3
    *   characters long.
    *
    * Expects:
    *   &ar    - array
    *   &len   - entry_len (with decimal places if numeric)
    *   &temp  - temp_entry
    *   &bot   - bot_index (first entry to sort)
    *   &top   - top_index (last entry to sort)
    *   ARYDSC - array_descending (optional)
    *
    * Returns:
    *   ARYERR - array_error *OFF
    *-----------------------------------------------------------------
    C           &arSRT      BEGSR
    *
    * Declare variables
    *
    C                       Z-ADD@I         @I       50
    C                       Z-ADD@O         @O       50
    C                       Z-ADD@NEXT      @NEXT    50
    C                       Z-ADD&BOT       @BOT     50
    C                       Z-ADD&TOP       @TOP     50
    C                       MOVE &temp      &temp &len
    C                       MOVE *OFF       ARYERR   1
    C                       MOVE ARYDSC     ARYDSC   1
    *
    * For first to last but one element
    *
    C           &top        SUB  1          @TOP
    C           &bot        DO   @TOP        @O
    *
    * .Compare with unsorted elements
    *
    C           @O          ADD  1          @NEXT
    C           @NEXT       DO   &top        @I
    *
    * ..Swap out of sequence elements
    *
    C           ARYDSC      IFNE *ON
    *
    C           &ar,@I      IFLT &ar,@O
```

Figure 7.1 ARYSRT Sort Array Template, continued

```
... 1 ...+... 2 ...+... 3 ...+... 4 ...+... 5 ...+... 6 ...+... 7 ...+... 8
C                         MOVE &ar,@O    &temp
C                         MOVE &ar,@I    &ar,@O
C                         MOVE &temp     &ar,@I
C                         ENDIF
 *
C                         ELSE
 *
C          &ar,@I         IFGT &ar,@O
C                         MOVE &ar,@O    &temp
C                         MOVE &ar,@I    &ar,@O
C                         MOVE &temp     &ar,@I
C                         ENDIF
 *
C                         ENDIF
 *
C                         ENDDO
 *
C                         ENDDO
 *
 * Clear optional arguments
 *
C                         MOVE *OFF      ARYDSC
 *
C                         ENDSR
```

Figure 7.2 ARYQSRT Quicksort Array Template

```
... 1 ...+... 2 ...+... 3 ...+... 4 ...+... 5 ...+... 6 ...+... 7 ...+... 8

 *-----------------------------------------------------------------
 * ARYQSRT    Quicksort array template
 *
 * Function:
 *   Very quickly sorts an array between the specified bottom
 *   and top entries in either ascending or descending order.
 *
 * Usage:
 *   Copy this template into your program and replace all
 *   &values listed below with your actual program variables.
 *   Syntax errors will occur if the array name is not 3
 *   characters long.
 *
 * Expects:
 *   &ar   - array
 *   &len   - entry_len (with decimal places if numeric)
 *   &pivot - pivot_entry
 *   &temp  - temp_entry
 *   &bot   - bot_index (first entry to sort)
 *   &top   - top_index (last entry to sort)
 *   ARYDSC - array_descending (optional)
 *
 * Returns:
 *   ARYERR - array_error on stack overflow (can't happen!)
```

Figure 7.2 ARYQSRT Quicksort Array Template, continued

```
... 1 ...+... 2 ...+... 3 ...+... 4 ...+... 5 ...+... 6 ...+... 7 ...+... 8
  *--------------------------------------------------------------
C           &arSRT     BEGSR
  *
  * Declare variables
  *
C                      Z-ADD0      @ARLVL  30
C                      MOVE @ARSTK @ARSTK250
C                      MOVE @ARSHF @ARSHF240
C                      MOVE @ARTOP @ARTOP 10
C                      Z-ADD25     @ARMAX  50
C                      Z-ADD@L     @L      50
C                      Z-ADD@M     @M      50
C                      Z-ADD@R     @R      50
C                      Z-ADD&bot   @BOT    50
C                      Z-ADD&top   @TOP    50
C                      MOVE &pivot &pivot&len
C                      MOVE &temp  &temp &len
C                      MOVE *OFF   ARYERR  1
C                      MOVE ARYDSC ARYDSC  1
  *
  * Sort the array
  *
C           *ON        DOWEQ*ON
  *
C                      SELEC
  *
  * .Something to sort in subset
  *
C           @BOT       WHLT @TOP
  *
C                      Z-ADD@BOT   @L
C                      Z-ADD@TOP   @R
  *
  * ..Get pivot from middle of subset
  *
C           @TOP       SUB  @BOT   @M
C                      MULT 0.5    @M
C                      ADD  @BOT   @M
C                      MOVE &ar,@M &pivot
  *
  * ..Partition the subset into two new subsets about the pivot:
  *     left subset <= pivot <= right subset
  *   (If descending array, reverse the order)
  *
C           @L         DOWLE@R
  *
  * ...Advance left and right pointers while elements in sequence
  *
C           ARYDSC     IFNE *ON
  *
C           &ar,@L     DOWLT&pivot
C                      ADD  1      @L
```

Figure 7.2 ARYQSRT Quicksort Array Template, continued

```
... 1 ...+... 2 ...+... 3 ...+... 4 ...+... 5 ...+... 6 ...+... 7 ...+... 8

C                       ENDDO
C           &ar,@R      DOWGT&pivot
C                       SUB  1          @R
C                       ENDDO
 *
C                       ELSE
 *
C           &ar,@L      DOWGT&pivot
C                       ADD  1          @L
C                       ENDDO
C           &ar,@R      DOWLT&pivot
C                       SUB  1          @R
C                       ENDDO
 *
C                       ENDIF
 *
 * ...Swap out of sequence elements
 *
C                       SELEC
C           @L          WHLT @R
C                       MOVE &ar,@L     &temp
C                       MOVE &ar,@R     &ar,@L
C                       MOVE &temp      &ar,@R
C                       ADD  1          @L
C                       SUB  1          @R
C           @L          WHEQ @R
C                       ADD  1          @L
C                       SUB  1          @R
C                       ENDSL
 *
C                       ENDDO
 *
 * ..Find subset with fewest entries for next pass:
 *     If right subset, save right and use left on next pass
 *     If left subset, save left and use right on next pass
 *
C           @R          IFGE @M
C                       MOVEL@L         @ARTOP
C                       MOVE @TOP       @ARTOP
C                       Z-ADD@BOT       @BOT
C                       Z-ADD@R         @TOP
C                       ELSE
C                       MOVEL@BOT       @ARTOP
C                       MOVE @R         @ARTOP
C                       Z-ADD@L         @BOT
C                       Z-ADD@TOP       @TOP
C                       ENDIF
 *
 * ..Push saved subset onto stack, or exit on overflow
 *
C           @ARLVL      IFLT @ARMAX
C                       ADD  1          @ARLVL
```

Figure 7.2 ARYQSRT Quicksort Array Template, continued

```
... 1 ...+... 2 ...+... 3 ...+... 4 ...+... 5 ...+... 6 ...+... 7 ...+... 8

C                      MOVEL@ARSTK     @ARSHF
C                      MOVE @ARSHF     @ARSTK
C                      MOVEL@ARTOP     @ARSTK
C                      ELSE
C                      MOVE *ON        ARYERR
C                      LEAVE
C                      ENDIF
 *
 * .Something to pop from stack
 *
C          @ARLVL      WHGT 0
 *
C                      MOVEL@ARTOP     @BOT
C                      MOVE @ARTOP     @TOP
 *
C                      SUB  1          @ARLVL
C                      MOVE @ARSTK     @ARSHF
C                      MOVEL@ARSHF     @ARSTK
C                      MOVEL@ARSTK     @ARTOP
 *
 * .Sort completed
 *
C                      OTHER
 *
C                      LEAVE
 *
C                      ENDSL
 *
C                      ENDDO
 *
 * Clear optional arguments
 *
C                      MOVE *OFF       ARYDSC
 *
C                      ENDSR
```

Searching Arrays

Chapter 8

Replace RPG's LOKUP op-code with the template in this chapter for a better and faster way to search arrays.

RPG's LOKUP op-code is notoriously slow with large arrays, and it can be a real resource hog when used frequently. To go with the sort techniques in the last chapter, we've written an RPG template, ARYSCH, which you can use instead of LOKUP. ARYSCH binary search is not only faster than LOKUP for large arrays, but ARYSCH also offers some additional functionality. With ARYSCH, you can limit the search to part of an array, search arrays in ascending or descending order, search for a partial match, and find the nearest element to the search argument when an exact match can't be found.

In the previous chapter, we showed you how to load and sort an array of item classes, CLS. We used two pointers to define the bottom and top of the data in the array, stored in the fields CLSBOT and CLSTOP. Now that the array is sorted, we can use the ARYSCH template to find any element in the array. First, you key the code to execute the search function:

```
 * Set value to search for in code somewhere
C                     MOVE '23'      ICCLS    P
 *
 * Search array for item class value in ICCLS field
 * and save index in C
C                     MOVE ICCLS     CLSARG
C                     EXSR CLSSCH
C                     Z-ADDARYIDX    C
C         ARYERR      IFEQ *OFF
  :                   .code for exact match
C                     ELSE
  :                   .code for nearest entry
C                     ENDIF
```

In this case, the CLSSCH search subroutine will attempt to find the item class value of 23. It will search and return either the index of the matching element in ARYIDX with ARYERR set off, or the index of the nearest element in ARYIDX with ARYERR set on.

Next, you copy the SCHARY template (Figure 8.1) into the source program at the end of the C-specs. Finally, you execute the following change commands on the SEU command line to replace the generic values in the template with the specific values for the item class array:

```
C   &ar      CLS      A
C   &len     ' 4 '    A
C   &arg     CLSARG   A
C   &comp    CLSCMP   A
C   &bot     CLSBOT   A
C   &top     CLSTOP   A
```

&ar is replaced by the array name CLS and creates a subroutine name of CLSSCH. As with the templates in the previous chapter, the array name must be 3 characters long; otherwise, code can be shifted to the left or right, resulting in syntax errors. &len is replaced by both the length of an element and its number of decimal places, as used in columns 49 to 52 of a C-spec. &arg is replaced by the class field CLSARG, which contains the search argument. &comp is replaced by the name of a work variable used to store an element from the array. &bot and &top are replaced by the CLSBOT and CLSTOP fields mentioned above.

By default, the ARYSCH template searches an array in ascending order. To search an array in descending order, you simply set field ARYDSC on before executing the search subroutine:

```
     *
     * Search array for item class in descending order
C                      MOVE ICCLS    CLSARG
C                      MOVE *ON      ARYDSC
C                      EXSR CLSSCH
C                      Z-ADDARYIDX   C
```

You should note that the ARYSCH template only works with sorted arrays, and that ARYDSC should only be specified if the array is actually sorted in descending sequence. Unpredictable results will occur if you fail to obey these guidelines.

You can modify the behavior of ARYSCH in a couple of ways to change the results it produces. First, because the ARYSCH template only searches the range of elements between ARYBOT and ARYTOP, you can adjust the values of these fields to limit the search to a subset of elements. Second, you can replace &len in the template with the first *n* characters of an element; this lets you search for a partial match rather than an exact match on the whole element. Finally, just as with the templates in the previous chapter, you can use ARYSCH as the basis for a function to search multiple-occurrence data structures or user spaces.

Figure 8.1 ARYSCH Search Array Template

```
... 1 ...+... 2 ...+... 3 ...+... 4 ...+... 5 ...+... 6 ...+... 7 ...+... 8

 *------------------------------------------------------------------
 * ARYSCH   Binary search array template
 *
 * Function:
 *   Search an array between the specified bottom and top
 *   entries for a value. The array may be in either ascending
 *   or descending sequence.
 *
 * Usage:
 *   Copy this template into your program and replace all
 *   &values listed below with your actual program variables.
 *   Syntax errors will occur if the array name is not 3
 *   characters long.
 *
 * Expects:
 *   &ar    - array (in ascending or descending order)
 *   &len   - arg_len (with decimal places if numeric)
 *   &arg   - search_arg
 *   &comp  - compare_val
 *   &bot   - bot_index (first entry to search)
 *   &top   - top_index (last entry to search)
 *   ARYDSC - array_descending (optional)
 *
 * Returns:
 *   ARYIDX - array_index of nearest element
 *   ARYERR - array_error if not exact match
 *------------------------------------------------------------------
C           &arSCH    BEGSR
 *
 * Declare variables
 *
C                     Z-ADD0      ARYIDX   50
C                     Z-ADD&bot   @BOT     50
C                     Z-ADD&top   @TOP     50
C                     Z-ADD0      @MID     50
C                     MOVE &arg   &arg   &len
C                     MOVE &comp  &comp  &len
C                     MOVE ARYDSC ARYDSC   1
C                     MOVE *ON    ARYERR   1
 *
 * Search array between subset of bottom to top
 *
C           @BOT      DOWLE@TOP
 *
 * .Get compare value from middle of subset
 *
C           @TOP      SUB  @BOT   @MID
C                     MULT 0.5    @MID
C                     ADD  @BOT   @MID
C                     MOVEL&ar,@MID &comp
 *
 * .Compare middle value to argument:
```

Figure 8.1 ARYSCH Search Array Template, continued

```
... 1 ...+... 2 ...+... 3 ...+... 4 ...+... 5 ...+... 6 ...+... 7 ...+... 8

    *     If less, use top half of subset on next pass
    *     If greater, use bottom half of subset on next pass
    *     Else equal, search complete
    *   (If descending array, reverse the order)
    *
C           ARYDSC    IFNE *ON
    *
C                     SELEC
C           &comp     WHLT &arg
C           @MID      ADD  1          @BOT
C           &comp     WHGT &arg
C           @MID      SUB  1          @TOP
C                     OTHER
C                     MOVE *OFF       ARYERR
C                     LEAVE
C                     ENDSL
    *
C                     ELSE
    *
C                     SELEC
C           &comp     WHLT &arg
C           @MID      SUB  1          @TOP
C           &comp     WHGT &arg
C           @MID      ADD  1          @BOT
C                     OTHER
C                     MOVE *OFF       ARYERR
C                     LEAVE
C                     ENDSL
    *
C                     ENDIF
    *
C                     ENDDO
    *
    * Return index of nearest element
    *
C                     Z-ADD@MID       ARYIDX
    *
    * Clear optional arguments
    *
C                     MOVE *OFF       ARYDSC
    *
C                     ENDSR
```

Multidimensional Arrays

Chapter 9

With the templates in this chapter, you can code multidimensional arrays in RPG.

As we have seen in the past couple of chapters, although RPG's built-in array-handling capabilities are limited, all you need is a little ingenuity to really make them sizzle. While most modern programming languages support at least three-dimensional arrays, RPG is still stuck in the first dimension. So in this chapter we introduce some simple templates you can use to handle two-dimensional (2D) and three-dimensional (3D) arrays:

ARYIDX2D	converts the x and y coordinates of a 2D array into a valid RPG array index (Figure 9.1).
ARYDIM2D	converts a valid RPG array index into the x and y coordinates of a 2D array (Figure 9.2).
ARYIDX3D	converts the x, y, and z coordinates of a 3D array into a valid RPG array index (Figure 9.3).
ARYDIM3D	converts a valid RPG array index into the x, y, and z coordinates of a 3D array (Figure 9.4).

In the following discussion, we focus on the templates for 3D arrays. All you need is a grasp of the basic concepts to use the templates for the 2D arrays, or to extend the principles to work with arrays of any dimension.

Let's see how to use the 3D array templates to implement a simple appointment-scheduling system. The system lets you schedule appointments for each hour of the working day, for each week of the year. To keep things simple, let's assume there are 10 working hours a day, 7 days a week, and 53 weeks per year. To code an array to store a description of each appointment requires 53 times 7 times 10 entries, or 3,710 total:

```
          *
          * Schedule array
          E                        SCD        3710 30
          *
          * x,y,z dimensions of schedule
          I              53                         C           SCDDWK
          I               7                         C           SCDDDY
          I              10                         C           SCDDHR
```

The SCD array holds the schedule, and the SCDDxx named constants
define the week, day, and hour dimensions of the array.

You can access any x, y, or z coordinate in the array using the
ARYIDX3D template (Figure 9.3). For example, to schedule an
appointment with Clark Kent on the first hour of day two of week 10,
you first code

```
          *
          * Schedule appointment
          C             'Clark'    CAT   'Kent':1  SCDNAM 30 P
          C                        Z-ADD10          SCDIWK
          C                        Z-ADD2           SCDIDY
          C                        Z-ADD1           SCDIHR
          C                        EXSR SCDIDX
          C             ARYERR     IFEQ *OFF
          C                        Z-ADDARYIDX      S         50
          C                        MOVE SCDNAM      SCD,S
          C                        ENDIF
```

The SCDIDX subroutine generated by the ARYIDX3D template
translates the week, day, and hour coordinates in the SCDIxx fields into
the array index, ARYIDX, which is used to load the appointment into the
SCD array.

Next, you copy the ARYIDX3D template (Figure 9.3) into the source
program at the end of the C-specs. Finally, you execute the following
change commands on the SEU command line to replace the generic
values in the template with the specific values for the schedule array:

```
          C  &ar       SCD      A
          C  &dim1     SCDDWK   A
          C  &dim2     SCDDDY   A
          C  &dim3     SCDDHR   A
          C  &idx1     SCDIWK   A
          C  &idx2     SCDIDY   A
          C  &idx3     SCDIHR   A
```

&ar is replaced by the array name SCD and creates a subroutine name of
SCDIDX. As in previous chapters, the array name must be 3 characters
long; otherwise, code can be shifted to the left or right, resulting in
syntax errors. &dim1 to &dim3 are replaced by the declared dimensions
of the SCD array, and &idx1 to &idx3 are replaced by the coordinates
for the requried array element.

Once the SCDIDX subroutine is in your program, you can access the SCD array in other ways. For example, you could add the following code to process each appointment in the schedule in sequence:

```
 *
 * Process schedule
C              1         DO   SCDDWK   SCDIWK
C              1         DO   SCDDDY   SCDIDY
C              1         DO   SCDDHR   SCDIHR
C                        EXSR SCDIDX
C                        Z-ADDARYIDX   S
C                        MOVE SCD,S     SCDNAM
 *                       .process entry
C                        ENDDO
C                        ENDDO
C                        ENDDO
```

The nested DO loops set the coordinates for each hour of each day of each week. Subroutine SCDIDX then translates the coordinates into array index ARYIDX, so the appointment in the schedule can be processed.

You can also translate the RPG array index into the x, y, and z coordinates for an array using the ARYDIM3D template (Figure 9.4). To find the first appointment in your schedule with Lois Lane, you first code

```
 *
 * Find appointment
C              'Lois'    CAT  'Lane':1  SCDNAM   P
C                        Z-ADD1         S
C              SCDNAM    LOKUP SCD,S                    99
 *
C              *IN99     IFEQ *ON
C                        Z-ADDS         ARYIDX
C                        EXSR SCDDIM
C              ARYERR    IFEQ *OFF
C                        .process appointment
C                        ENDIF
C                        ENDIF
```

The SCDDIM subroutine translates the array index ARYIDX into the SCDIxx coordinates for the week, day, and year. Just as with ARYIDX3D, you copy the ARYDIM3D template (Figure 9.4) into the source program at the end of the C-specs and perform the same SEU change commands to generate the finished version of the SCDDIM subroutine.

Figure 9.1 ARYIDX2D Return Array Index to 2D Array Template

```
... 1 ...+... 2 ...+... 3 ...+... 4 ...+... 5 ...+... 6 ...+... 7 ...+... 8

     *------------------------------------------------------------------
     * ARYIDX2D   Return array index to 2D array template
     *
     * Function:
     *   Calculates the array index to a 2 dimensional array from
     *   the indexes to each of the individual dimensions.
     *
     * Usage:
     *   Copy this template into your program and replace all
     *   &values listed below with your actual program variables.
     *   Syntax errors will occur if the array name is not 3
     *   characters long.
     *
     * Expects:
     *   &ar    - array
     *   &dim1  - array_dim1_size
     *   &dim2  - array_dim2_size
     *   &idx1  - array_index1
     *   &idx2  - array_index2
     *
     * Returns:
     *   ARYIDX - array_index
     *   ARYERR - array_error on out of bounds index
     *------------------------------------------------------------------
     C           &arIDX    BEGSR
     *
     C           @&arD1    IFEQ 0
     C                     Z-ADD&dim2      @&arD2  50
     C           @&arD2    MULT &dim1      @&arD1  50
     C                     ENDIF
     *
     C           &idx1     IFLT 1
     C           &idx1     ORGT &dim1
     C           &idx2     ORLT 1
     C           &idx2     ORGT &dim2
     *
     C                     Z-ADD0          ARYIDX  50
     C                     MOVE *ON        ARYERR  1
     *
     C                     ELSE
     *
     C           &idx1     SUB  1          @&arI1  50
     C                     MULT @&arD2     @&arI1
     *
     C           &idx2     ADD  @&arI1     ARYIDX
     C                     MOVE *OFF       ARYERR
     *
     C                     ENDIF
     *
     C                     ENDSR
```

Figure 9.2 ARYDIM2D Return Dimensional Indexes to 2D Array Template

```
 ... 1 ...+... 2 ...+... 3 ...+... 4 ...+... 5 ...+... 6 ...+... 7 ...+... 8

  *------------------------------------------------------------------
  * ARYDIM2D   Return dimensional indexes to 2D array template
  *
  * Function:
  *   Calculates the indexes to each of the individual dimensions
  *   to a 2 dimensional array from the array index.
  *
  * Usage:
  *   Copy this template into your program and replace all
  *   &values listed below with your actual program variables.
  *   Syntax errors will occur if the array name is not 3
  *   characters long.
  *
  * Expects:
  *   &ar    - array
  *   &dim1  - array_dim1_size
  *   &dim2  - array_dim2_size
  *   ARYIDX - array_index
  *
  * Returns:
  *   &idx1  - array_index1
  *   &idx2  - array_index2
  *   ARYERR - array_error on out of bounds index
  *------------------------------------------------------------------
C           &arDIM    BEGSR
  *
C                     Z-ADDARYIDX     ARYIDX  50
C                     MOVE *OFF       ARYERR  1
  *
C           @&arD1    IFEQ 0
C                     Z-ADD&dim2      @&arD2  50
C           @&arD2    MULT &dim1      @&arD1  50
C                     ENDIF
  *
C           ARYIDX    IFLT 1
C           ARYIDX    ORGT @&arD1
  *
C                     MOVE *ON        ARYERR
C                     Z-ADD0          &idx1
C                     Z-ADD0          &idx2
C                     Z-ADD0          &idx3
  *
C                     ELSE
  *
C           ARYIDX    DIV  @&arD2     @idx1
C                     MVR             @idx2
C           &idx2     IFEQ 0
C                     Z-ADD@&arD2     @idx2
C                     ELSE
C                     ADD  1          &idx1
C                     ENDIF
  *
```

Figure 9.2 ARYDIM2D Return Dimensional Indexes to 2D Array Template, continued

```
... 1 ...+... 2 ...+... 3 ...+... 4 ...+... 5 ...+... 6 ...+... 7 ...+... 8

C                       ENDIF
 *
C                       ENDSR
```

Figure 9.3 ARYIDX3D Return Array Index to 3D Array Template

```
... 1 ...+... 2 ...+... 3 ...+... 4 ...+... 5 ...+... 6 ...+... 7 ...+... 8

 *-------------------------------------------------------------------
 * ARYIDX3D   Return array index to 3D array template
 *
 * Function:
 *   Calculates the array index to a 3 dimensional array from
 *   the indexes to each of the individual dimensions.
 *
 * Usage:
 *   Copy this template into your program and replace all
 *   &values listed below with your actual program variables.
 *   Syntax errors will occur if the array name is not 3
 *   characters long.
 *
 * Expects:
 *   &ar    - array
 *   &dim1  - array_dim1_size
 *   &dim2  - array_dim2_size
 *   &dim3  - array_dim3_size
 *   &idx1  - array_index1
 *   &idx2  - array_index2
 *   &idx3  - array_index3
 *
 * Returns:
 *   ARYIDX - array_index
 *   ARYERR - array_error on out of bounds index
 *-------------------------------------------------------------------
C           &arIDX    BEGSR
 *
C           @&arD1    IFEQ 0
C                     Z-ADD&dim3    @&arD3  50
C           @&arD3    MULT &dim2    @&arD2  50
C           @&arD2    MULT &dim1    @&arD1  50
C                     ENDIF
 *
C           &idx1     IFLT 1
C           &idx1     ORGT &dim1
C           &idx2     ORLT 1
C           &idx2     ORGT &dim2
C           &idx3     ORLT 1
C           &idx3     ORGT &dim3
 *
C                     Z-ADD0        ARYIDX  50
C                     MOVE *ON      ARYERR  1
 *
```

Figure 9.3 ARYIDX3D Return Array Index to 3D Array Template, continued

```
... 1 ...+... 2 ...+... 3 ...+... 4 ...+... 5 ...+... 6 ...+... 7 ...+... 8

C                     ELSE
 *
C           &idx1     SUB  1         @&arI1  50
C                     MULT @&arD2    @&arI1
 *
C           &idx2     SUB  1         @&arI2  50
C                     MULT @&arD3    @&arI2
 *
C           &idx3     ADD  @&arI2    ARYIDX
C                     ADD  @&arI1    ARYIDX
C                     MOVE *OFF      ARYERR
 *
C                     ENDIF
 *
C                     ENDSR
```

Figure 9.4 ARYDIM3D Return Dimensional Indexes to 3D Array Template

```
... 1 ...+... 2 ...+... 3 ...+... 4 ...+... 5 ...+... 6 ...+... 7 ...+... 8

 *----------------------------------------------------------------
 * ARYDIM3D - Return dimensional indexes to 3D array template
 *
 * Function:
 *   Calculates the indexes to each of the individual dimensions
 *   to a 3-dimensional array from the array index.
 *
 * Usage:
 *   Copy this template into your program and replace all
 *   &values listed below with your actual program variables.
 *   Syntax errors will occur if the array name is not 3
 *   characters long.
 *
 * Expects:
 *   &ar     - array
 *   &dim1   - array_dim1_size
 *   &dim2   - array_dim2_size
 *   &dim3   - array_dim3_size
 *   ARYIDX  - array_index
 *
 * Returns:
 *   &idx1   - array_index1
 *   &idx2   - array_index2
 *   &idx3   - array_index3
 *   ARYERR  - array_error on out of bounds index
 *----------------------------------------------------------------
C           &arDIM    BEGSR
 *
C                     Z-ADDARYIDX    ARYIDX  50
C                     MOVE *OFF      ARYERR  1
 *
C           @&arD1    IFEQ 0
```

```
C                       Z-ADD&dim3      @&arD3  50
C           @&arD3      MULT &dim2      @&arD2  50
C           @&arD2      MULT &dim1      @&arD1  50
C                       ENDIF
 *
C           ARYIDX      IFLT 1
C           ARYIDX      ORGT @&arD1
 *
C                       MOVE *ON        ARYERR
C                       Z-ADD0          &idx1
C                       Z-ADD0          &idx2
C                       Z-ADD0          &idx3
 *
C                       ELSE
 *
C           ARYIDX      DIV  @&arD2     @idx1
C                       MVR             @idx2
C           &idx2       IFEQ 0
C                       Z-ADD@&arD2     @idx2
C                       ELSE
C                       ADD  1          &idx1
C                       ENDIF
 *
C           &idx2       DIV  @&arD3     @idx2
C                       MVR             @idx3
C           &idx3       IFEQ 0
C                       Z-ADD@&arD3     @idx3
C                       ELSE
C                       ADD  1          &idx2
C                       ENDIF
 *
C                       ENDIF
 *
C                       ENDSR
```

Dynamically
Determining Keypresses

Chapter 10

*Minimize indicator
dependency and make
your code more readable
by using the AID byte to
dynamically determine
keypresses in interactive
RPG programs, and to
determine other
keypresses beyond the
function keys.*

Like disk and printer files, display files also have a file information data structure. This data structure is defined in member WSDS, as shown in Figure 10.1. This abbreviated data structure contains all the relevant display-file-related values available in the file information data structure. For a detailed listing of what else is in this data structure, see the IBM *AS/400 RPG/400 Reference* (SC09-1817-00) and the *IBM AS/400 Data Management Guide* (SC41-3710-00).

Two of the most useful functions of the display file I/O feedback area are to determine the most recent key the operator pressed and to determine the current cursor position (discussed in Chapter 12).

RPG and DDS use indicators almost exclusively to communicate with each other. To minimize that indicator dependence between RPG and DDS, and to make your RPG easier to read, use the Attention Indicator byte (AID) to dynamically determine what key the operator presses in your RPG programs.

The AID byte is a 1-byte hexadecimal value reported back to your RPG program by way of the display file's I/O feedback area. By adding a data structure name in the display file's F-spec, and using two /COPY files, you can then simply compare the AID byte to program constants to determine what key the operator pressed. Figure 10.2 shows WSCONS, the member that contains the named constants used to compare against the AID byte to determine the most recent keypress.

Figure 10.3 shows a snippet of a sample RPG program using these two members. Note that Figure 10.3 defines the name of the display file I/O feedback data structure as WSDS (because that is its name in the WSDS /COPY member) in the continuation line area of the F-spec. This continuation line definition of the file information data structure is required when using the /COPY members shown in this chapter.

For even more readable code, you may want to extend this technique to actually map key assignments to more meaningful keypress names. For example, Figure 10.4 shows several of the most-used CUA key assignments mapped to named constants. Now, rather than checking for F3 or F5, your code can check for EXIT or REFRSH (Refresh) keystrokes. You can extend Figure 10.4 to include your shop's most common key assignments for user-defined keys. Be aware that, if you use Figure 10.4 as provided (unlike most of the members provided in this book), it does not use unique prefixes on its field names. We did this because we think a named constant of CANCEL makes infinitely more sense than WSCNCL — using contrived prefixes almost defeats the purpose of Figure 10.4's technique, given RPG's six-character field-name limits. If you use Figure 10.4 in your code, scour it carefully for field naming conflicts with your production code.

The next chapter shows how you can use the WSDS module for help with cursor positioning.

Figure 10.1 WSDS RPG /COPY Member

```
... 1 ...+... 2 ...+... 3 ...+... 4 ...+... 5 ...+... 6 ...+... 7 ...+... 8

 *----------------------------------------------------------------
 * WSDS - Workstation display file info
 *
 * WSKEY  - Keypress value
 * WSCSR  - Binary cursor location
 * WSSFRN - Current subfile relative record number
 * WSSRLR - Current lowest subfile relative record number displayed
 * WSSFTR - Total number of records in a subfile
 * WSWCSR - Binary cursor location in a window
 *
 * Requires:
 *   WSDS data structure be named in display F-spec KINFDS
 *   continuation area of calling program.
 *----------------------------------------------------------------
IWSDS         DS
I                                       369 369 WSKEY
I                                     B 370 3710WSCSR
I                                     B 376 3770WSSFRN
I                                     B 378 3790WSSRLR
I                                     B 380 3810WSSFTR
I                                     B 382 3830WSWCSR
```

Figure 10.2 WSCONS RPG /COPY Member

```
... 1 ...+... 2 ...+... 3 ...+... 4 ...+... 5 ...+... 6 ...+... 7 ...+... 8


  *------------------------------------------------------------------
  * WSCONS - Named hexadecimal constants for function keys
  *------------------------------------------------------------------
I               X'31'                 C          WSF01
I               X'32'                 C          WSF02
I               X'33'                 C          WSF03
I               X'34'                 C          WSF04
I               X'35'                 C          WSF05
I               X'36'                 C          WSF06
I               X'37'                 C          WSF07
I               X'38'                 C          WSF08
I               X'39'                 C          WSF09
I               X'3A'                 C          WSF10
I               X'3B'                 C          WSF11
I               X'3C'                 C          WSF12
I               X'B1'                 C          WSF13
I               X'B2'                 C          WSF14
I               X'B3'                 C          WSF15
I               X'B4'                 C          WSF16
I               X'B5'                 C          WSF17
I               X'B6'                 C          WSF18
I               X'B7'                 C          WSF19
I               X'B8'                 C          WSF20
I               X'B9'                 C          WSF21
I               X'BA'                 C          WSF22
I               X'BB'                 C          WSF23
I               X'BC'                 C          WSF24
I               X'BD'                 C          WSCLR
I               X'F1'                 C          WSENTR
I               X'F3'                 C          WSHELP
I               X'F4'                 C          WSPGUP
I               X'F5'                 C          WSPGDN
I               X'F6'                 C          WSPRT
```

Figure 10.3 Example RPG Snippet Using AID Byte and /COPY Members

```
... 1 ...+... 2 ...+... 3 ...+... 4 ...+... 5 ...+... 6 ...+... 7 ...+... 8


  * Note KINFDS continuation line naming WSDS data structure below
FWORKST  CF  E                    WORKSTN    KINFDS WSDS
  *
 /COPY WSDS
 /COPY WSCONS
   :
C          SHOFMT     BEGSR
C                     EXFMTFMTNAME                  99
C                     SELEC
C          WSKEY      WHEQ WSF03
   :
   :                  F3 keypress action here
   :
C          WSKEY      WHEQ WSF05
```

Figure 10.3 Example RPG Snippet Using AID Byte and /COPY Members, continued

```
... 1 ...+... 2 ...+... 3 ...+... 4 ...+... 5 ...+... 6 ...+... 7 ...+... 8

      :
      :                   F3 keypress action here
      :
C              WSKEY       WHEQ WSENTR
      :
      :                   Enter keypress action here
      :
C                          ENDSL
C                          ENDSR
```

Figure 10.4 CUA Keypress Mnemonic Constants

```
... 1 ...+... 2 ...+... 3 ...+... 4 ...+... 5 ...+... 6 ...+... 7 ...+... 8

 *--------------------------------------------------------------
 * WSCUA - Named CUA hex constants
 *--------------------------------------------------------------
I              X'31'                   C        HELP
I              X'33'                   C        EXIT
I              X'34'                   C        PROMPT
I              X'35'                   C        REFRSH
I              X'36'                   C        CREATE
I              X'37'                   C        RETRV
I              X'3C'                   C        CANCEL
I              X'B5'                   C        TOP
I              X'B6'                   C        BOTTOM
I              X'B7'                   C        LEFT
I              X'B8'                   C        RIGHT
I              X'BB'                   C        OPTION
I              X'BC'                   C        KEYS
```

Getting and Setting the Cursor Position

Chapter 11

This technique dynamically gets and sets the cursor row and column position for your interactive programs.

The previous chapter showed how to use the display file information data structure to determine keypresses, but it can also be used to determine the current cursor position. The information data structure reports the cursor row and column position as a single binary value in positions 370-371. Dividing this value by 256 yields the current cursor row position, and the remainder of that division yields the current cursor column position. Using the WSDS RPG /COPY module from Chapter 10, the following RPG snippet shows how to determine the cursor position:

```
FWORKST   CF  E                         WORKSTN      KINFDS WSDS
 *
I/COPY WSDS
 *
   :
 *
C                         EXFMTFMTNAME                    99
C* Determine cursor row and column position
C            WSCSR      DIV  256        #CSROW  20
C                       MVR             #CSCOL  30
```

Note that a three-digit integer is used to hold the column position in case a 132-column workstation is being used. Remember also that using the WSDS /COPY member requires that the display file F-spec specify a KINFDS continuation line to name the WSDS data structure for the display file being used.

In addition to determining the cursor position on the screen, the file information data structure can also be used to determine the cursor position in an active window. The same technique shown here applies, but for windows you must use the WSWCSR field (in position 383 and in position 383 of the file information data structure). The coordinates reported by this field are always relative to the upper left-hand corner of the window.

If you need to know more than just the cursor position, the DDS keyword RTNCSRLOC returns not only the cursor position, but also the name of the display format and the field on which the cursor is located. It can even tell you the cursor's position in the field. You specify the RTNCSRLOC keyword in the format shown in Figure 11.1.

You must always specify RTNCSRLOC with two or three variables that refer to hidden fields in the display file, as the figure shows. OS/400's display management routines place the cursor position feedback information into these fields. Field CSRRCD will contain the name of the record format within which the cursor is located, and field CSRFLD will contain the name of the field. If the cursor is not located in a valid record or field, the respective field will be blank.

The third return variable used with RTNCSRLOC (&CSRPOS) is optional. If your application needs to know where the cursor is located within a field on the screen, you can use this keyword to return that information. As a result of the coding in Figure 11.1, for example, if the user presses Enter while the cursor is in the third position of the CUSNBR field, the RTNCSRLOC feature will return CSRRCD with the value FMT01, CSRFLD with the value CUSNBR, and CSRPOS with the value 3.

Be sure to define each of these fields (CSRRCD, CSRFLD, and CSRPOS) with the same data types and lengths as the examples shown. Also, note that you precede each variable with an ampersand (&) when you specify it as an argument in the RTNCSRLOC keyword, similar to the way you specify variables in a CL program.

Besides finding out where your cursor came from, you can tell it where to go. The DDS cursor-positioning function, DSPATR(PC), has been around since the early days, of course. But you may not know about the more recent CSRLOC (cursor location) DDS keyword, which lets you specify the coordinates where you want the cursor to appear when your program displays the screen. In Figure 11.1, CSRLOC specifies two fields, ROW and COL, which refer to hidden 3-byte, zoned-decimal fields in the display file. You put into these fields the values of the row and the column where you want the cursor to be when your program displays the screen. Notice that you can set an option indicator (e.g., indicator 05 in the figure) if you want to condition the cursor location,

---

but you can only specify it once for each record format. If both CSRLOC and DSPATR(PC) are in effect for a single output operation to a display, CSRLOC takes precedence over DSPATR(PC).

For applications that use subfiles, there are analogous cursor manipulation functions that apply especially to subfiles. The SFLCSRRRN keyword (available in V2R2 and greater) returns to your program the relative record number of the subfile record in which your cursor is positioned. SFLRCDNBR(CURSOR) lets you specify cursor positioning on a specific subfile record.

Figure 11.1 DDS to Set the Cursor Location

```
... 1 ...+... 2 ...+... 3 ...+... 4 ...+... 5 ...+... 6 ...+... 7 ...+... 8

A              RFMT01
A                                               RTNCSRLOC(&CSRRCD +
A                                                         &CSRFLD +
A                                                         &CSRPOS)
A    05                                         CSRLOC(ROW COL)
A              CSRRCD        10A   H
A              CSRFLD        10A   H
A              CSRPOS         4S  0H
A              ROW            3S  0H
A              COL            3S  0H
A              OPTION         1A   B    1    2
A              CUSNBR         7S  0B    1    5
```

Using Named Indicators with Interactive Programs

Use this indicator "swindle" to make your interactive RPG programs more readable and easier to maintain.

RPG almost goes out of its way to make itself hard to read. Its painfully short field names and rigid columns are trouble enough, but its dogged reliance on indicators to communicate with DDS panels is especially frustrating. Here is a technique you can use to map meaningful (meaningful within RPG's six-character definition of meaningful!) names to screen-attribute and user-input indicators.

This technique relies on two include members, INDDS (Figure 12.1) and INGETPUT (Figure 12.2). INDDS defines a 99-byte data structure used to map *IN indicator values. INGETPUT provides two short subroutines to tranfer indicator values between INDDS's data structure and RPG's *IN indicator array.

To use this technique, include the INDDS member somewhere in your RPG program's I-specs and the INGETPUT member somewhere in the subroutine section of your C-specs. To "map" indicator positions to field names, add additional I-specs immediately under the INDDS /COPY statement. In the example below, nine data structure subfields provide field names for subfile events, keystroke events, and screen attributes that can occur in the program.

```
    /COPY INDDS
I                                       33  33 #SFTOP
I                                       34  34 #SFBOT
I                                       60  60 #PROT
I                                       80  80 #SFLCR
I                                       81  81 #SFDSP
I                                       82  82 #SFEND
I                                       90  90 #POSTO
I                                       91  91 #PGUP
I                                       92  92 #PGDN
```

For example, #PROT is mapped to indicator 60, which is used in the DDS to protect some input fields when a given circumstance occurs. By using this technique, you simply set the value of #PROT without needing to worry about what actual indicator value is being referenced.

After including these members, all you need to do to put them to work is, immediately before any workstation output, call the INDPUT subroutine to transfer indicator values from INDDS's indicator structure to the *IN array; and immediately after any workstation output, call the INDGET subroutine to transfer *IN indicator values into INDDS's indicator structure.

Notice in the code below that *ON is used to set the #PROT mapped indicator on. To set values in the INDDS data structure, you can use RPG's *ON and *OFF figurative constants. These constants simply move a 1 or a 0 into a character-based field; and they can be used with any character-based field, not just RPG indicators.

```
     /COPY INDDS
I                                              33   33 #SFTOP
I                                              34   34 #SFBOT
I                                              60   60 #PROT
I                                              80   80 #SFLCR
I                                              81   81 #SFDSP
I                                              82   82 #SFEND
I                                              90   90 #POSTO
I                                              91   91 #PGUP
I                                              92   92 #PGDN
     :
    *------------------------------------------------------------
    * DSPLST - Display list
    *------------------------------------------------------------
C           DSPLST     BEGSR
    *
    * Manually set any mapped indicators as needed here.
    * In this example, an indicator used to control the
    * protect-input attribute of some fields is enabled,
    * if the condition calls for it.
    *
C           COND       IFEQ PROTEC
C                      MOVE *ON        #PROT
C                      ELSE
C                      MOVE *OFF       #PROT
C                      ENDIF
    *
C                      EXSR INDPUT
C                      EXFMTSFLCTL
C                      EXSR INDGET
     :
C           *INKE      CASEQ*ON        RFSLST
C           *INKF      CASEQ*ON        PRCOPT
C           *INKL      CASEQ*ON        CNLPGM
C           #POSTO     CASEQ*ON        INZLST
```

```
C               #PGDN     CASEQ*ON      PAGEDN
C               #PGUP     CASEQ*ON      PAGEUP
C                         ENDCS
  :
 *
 * Subsequent routines could check the values of other
 * mapped values to test for specific actions. For example,
 * #SFTOP and #SFBOT could be checked to see if the subfile
 * is positioned at the top or the bottom of the subfile.
 *
  :
C                         ENDSR
  :
 /COPY INGETPUT
  :
```

Figure 12.1 INDDS Indicator /COPY Module

```
... 1 ...+... 2 ...+... 3 ...+... 4 ...+... 5 ...+... 6 ...+... 7 ...+... 8

 *-------------------------------------------------------------------
 * INDDS   -   Array of user indicators (corresponds to *IN).
 *
 * Function:
 *    Used with GETIND and PUTIND (in member INGETPUT) to get and
 *    put values in *IN indicator array.
 *-------------------------------------------------------------------
 *
IINDDS       DS
I I              '0000000000000000000-   1  99 #IND
I                '0000000000000000000-
I                '0000000000000000000-
I                '0000000000000000000-
I                '0000000000000000000'
```

Figure 12.2 INGETPUT Indicator Get and Put /COPY Module

```
... 1 ...+... 2 ...+... 3 ...+... 4 ...+... 5 ...+... 6 ...+... 7 ...+... 8

 *-------------------------------------------------------------------
 * INGETPUT   -   Get or put indicator array.
 *
 * Function:
 *    These two subroutines get and put indicator values in *IN.
 *    It is usually used for screen attribute control or to
 *    manage user input with interactive programs.
 *
 *-------------------------------------------------------------------
 * INDGET - Get indicator values from *IN
 *-------------------------------------------------------------------
C          INDGET    BEGSR
 *
C                    MOVEA*IN      INDDS
 *
C                    ENDSR
```

Figure 12.2 INGETPUT Indicator Get and Put /COPY Module, continued

```
... 1 ...+... 2 ...+... 3 ...+... 4 ...+... 5 ...+... 6 ...+... 7 ...+... 8

      *
      *----------------------------------------------------------------
      * INDPUT - Put indicator values into *IN
      *----------------------------------------------------------------
     C          INDPUT    BEGSR
      *
     C                    MOVEAINDDS      *IN
      *
     C                    ENDSR
```

Using a Message Subfile to Display Error Messages

Chapter 13

Enhance your programs' messaging capabilities by harnessing the power of message subfiles and the program message queue.

Taking advantage of OS/400's superb messaging facilities to display program messages adds a level of professionalism to your applications and makes it easy to externalize (and therefore reuse) program messages. Because second-level help is built into this messaging system, messages displayed this way easily provide an increased level of information to your users. Also, depending on your design criteria, using the program message queue makes it possible to send more than one error message at a time to a program message queue. As illustrated with the code provided in this chapter, though, you can limit the number of error messages the operator sees at once (we recommend displaying messages one at a time).

This chapter shows how to harness the power of program message queues to provide this messaging facility for your application programs. Figure 13.1 shows an example screen displaying one message from the program message queue. The plus sign near the right edge of the screen indicates there are other messages for the operator to see (these additional messages can be seen using the Page Up and Page Down keys). To display second-level Help, all the operator needs to do is put the cursor anywhere on the message and press the Help key; any available second-level Help will then be displayed.

The program, MSGERR, which displays the screen shown in Figure 13.1, is shown in Figure 13.2; and the display file DDS, MSGERRD, is shown in Figure 13.3. MSGERR makes substantial use of previously referenced /COPY members, and this chapter adds three new ones: MSGDS, an RPG I-spec /COPY member (Figure 13.4) that provides several messaging-related variables and constants; and MSGSND and MSGCLR, RPG C-spec /COPY members (Figure 13.5 and Figure 13.6) that provide subroutines to send and clear program messages from a program message queue (these subroutines call two OS/400 message-related APIs). To use these two members, include MSGDS somewhere in your program's I-specs and include MSGSND and MSGCLR somewhere in the subroutine section of your program's C-specs.

You'll also need to include two message subfile-related record formats in your program's display file DDS. These two record formats are shown in the shaded area in Figure 13.3 and should be copied "as is" to your display file DDS — there is nothing application-specific in them. Although indicator 99 is referenced with the SFLEND keyword, the code works regardless of the status of indicator 99 (the SLFEND keyword requires an option indicator, but as coded here doesn't use it). The DDS keyword SFLPGMQ (Subfile program message queue) links the subfile coded in these DDS specs to the program message queue of the program specified in the variable PSPGM (which is obtained from the program information data structure, defined in /COPY member PGMSDS — see Chapter 2).

It is very important that any display file formats displayed following the error message subfile have the record-level DDS keyword OVERLAY associated with them; if they don't, the message subfile area will be cleared before the operator sees it.

In your RPG program, just before a display file write operation (either with the WRITE or EXFMT operation codes), write the MSGCTL display file subfile record (shown being written in the shaded lines in Figure 13.2). If no messages are in the program message queue, none are displayed; otherwise, messages in the queue will be displayed one at a time, and you can use the Page Up and Page Down keys to display others. When messages are displayed in this way, the keyboard isn't locked and the cursor remains at its current input field position. Note that it is very important that any display file formats displayed after the error message subfile has been displayed have the record-level DDS keyword OVERLAY associated with them; if they don't, the message subfile area will be cleared before the operator sees it.

In program MSGERR, the SNDM subroutine (called when F13 is pressed) sends three messages to the program message queue. Generally, you will condition sending messages on some kind of input-verifying code; in this example, MSGERR unconditionally sends three messages to simply illustrate the concept. To send a message, you need to provide the following parameters:

MSGF	Name of the message file from which messages should be displayed.
MSGL	Name of the message file library.
MSGTYP	Message type. You'll almost always send *DIAG messages, which is indicated with the MSDIAG constant.
MSGQ	Program message queue. You can send messages to the current program queue or to the external message queue. In this case, you'll want to send them to the current

	program queue, which is indicated with the MSCURQ constant.
MSGST	Program call stack. This is a numeric value that indicates how many programs up the invocation stack messages should be sent. For example, to send them to program A from program A, use a MSGSTK value of 0 (which is indicated with the constant value of MSCSTK). If program A called program B, and you wanted program B to send messages to program A's queue, you would use a call stack value of 1 (as indicated by the constant MSPSTK). Only values 0 and 1 have constants provided for them, but you may need to code other level values depending on how nested your programs get.
MSGID	Message ID. This is the 7-character message ID of the OS/400 message to display.
MSGTXT	Variable message text. If the message uses variable text, this variable lets you provide up to 79 characters of variable message text.
MSGLEN	Length of variable message text. This variable must define the length of the variable message text provided. For messages that don't provide variable text, set MSGTXT to blanks and MSGLEN to zero.

Examine subroutine SNDM closely in Figure 13.2 to see how these variables are being displayed to send program messages.

To remove messages from its program message queue, MSGERR simply calls subroutine MSGCLR (shown in the /COPY member MSGCLR in Figure 13.6) when F14 is pressed. This routine is intended to be called from the program from which you want to remove messages; thus, you don't need to specify the program message queue or program call stack for this routine. While the example program unconditionally removes the messages on a simple keystroke, your application logic will generally remove them after field validation and after the operator has seen the messages and corrected the errors indicated.

The only other thing you need to do to display program messages is to have messages to display. For that, you can use the WRKMSGD command to interactively maintain a message file. Alternatively, you can use the ADDMSGD command (as shown on the next page) to add messages one at a time to a message file.

```
ADDMSGD MSGID( USR0001 )
        MSGF( *LIBL/USRERRS )
        MSG( 'This is the first message using variable data:
        SECLVL( 'This is the first message second level help
        FMT( ( *CHAR 8 ) )
```

MSGERR is only 78 lines long; yet when all the /COPY members are included, MSGERR expands to more than 400 lines of code!

One last general note about program MSGERR (Figure 13.2): Note how this program illustrates the concept of building programs quickly from proven, tested chunks of reusable code. MSGERR is only 78 lines long; yet when all the /COPY members are included (automatically, by the RPG compiler), MSGERR expands to more than 400 lines of code. As you can see, MSGERR was easier to write, and easier to test, using the /COPY modules, than it would have been to write all 400+ lines from scratch. In this case, less than 20 percent of the RPG required to write a complete program had to be written from scratch.

Figure 13.1 Example Screen Showing a Message Displayed from the Program Message Queue

Input field.................. ▌_____

F3=Exit F13=Send messages F14=Clear messages
This is the first message using variable data: Hi there

Figure 13.2 Example Program Using an Error Message Subfile

```
... 1 ...+... 2 ...+... 3 ...+... 4 ...+... 5 ...+... 6 ...+... 7 ...+... 8

 /COPY CTLWDMP
 *
FMSGERRD CF   E                        WORKSTN      KINFDS WSDS
 *
 /COPY ERRDS
 /COPY MSGDS
 /COPY PGMSDS
 /COPY STDTYPES
 /COPY WSCONS
 /COPY WSCUA
 /COPY WSDS
 *
C                       MOVEL*OFF      EXTPGM
 *
C           EXTPGM      DOWNE*ON
 *
 * Write error message subfile
C                       WRITEMSGCTL
 *
 * Write and read workstation format:
C                       EXFMTSCREEN
 *
C                       SELEC
 * Stop when EXIT key is pressed
C           WSKEY       WHEQ EXIT
C                       MOVEL*ON       EXTPGM
 *
 * Send three messages to program queue
C           WSKEY       WHEQ WSF13
C                       EXSR SNDM
 *
 * Clear all messages from program queue
C           WSKEY       WHEQ WSF14
C                       EXSR MSGCLR
 *
C                       ENDSL
 *
C                       ENDDO
 *
C                       MOVEL*ON       *INLR
 *
C                       RETRN
 *
 *
C           *INZSR      BEGSR
 *
C           *LIKE       DEFN #BOOL     EXTPGM
 *
C                       ENDSR
 *
 *
```

Figure 13.2 Example Program Using an Error Message Subfile, continued

```
... 1 ...+... 2 ...+... 3 ...+... 4 ...+... 5 ...+... 6 ...+... 7 ...+... 8

C           SNDM        BEGSR
 *
 * Set message file and library
C                       MOVEL'USRERRS' MSGF      P
C                       MOVEL'*LIBL'   MSGL      p
 * Set message type
C                       MOVELMSDIAG    MSGTYP    P
 * Set message queue and stack
C                       MOVELMSCURQ    MSGQ      P
C                       Z-ADDMSCSTK    MSGSTK
 *
 * Send USR0001 with program name as variable data:
C                       MOVEL'USR0001' MSGID     P
C                       MOVEL'Hi there'MSGTXT    P
C                       Z-ADD8         MSGLEN
C                       EXSR MSGSND
 *
 * Send USR0002 (no variable data):
C                       MOVEL'USR0002' MSGID
C                       EXSR MSGSND
 *
 * Send USR0003 (no variable data):
C                       MOVEL'USR0003' MSGID
C                       EXSR MSGSND
 *
C                       ENDSR
 *
 /COPY MSGSND
 /COPY MSGCLR
 /COPY PSSR
```

Figure 13.3 Example DDS to Implement an Error Message Subfile

```
... 1 ...+... 2 ...+... 3 ...+... 4 ...+... 5 ...+... 6 ...+... 7 ...+... 8

A                                     DSPSIZ( 24 80 *DS3 )
A                                     PRINT
 *--------------------------------------------------------------------
 * Input record
 *--------------------------------------------------------------------
A          R SCREEN
A                                     CF03 CF13 CF14
A                                     OVERLAY
 *
A                              4  8'Input field...................'
A          WKNAME       24  B  4 40
A                             23  2'F3=Exit'
A                             23 11'F13=Send messages'
A                             23 30'F14=Clear messages'
 *--------------------------------------------------------------------
 * Error message subfile
 *--------------------------------------------------------------------
```

Figure 13.3 Example DDS to Implement an Error Message Subfile, continued

```
... 1 ...+... 2 ...+... 3 ...+... 4 ...+... 5 ...+... 6 ...+... 7 ...+... 8
 A           R MSGSFL                      SFL
 A                                         SFLMSGRCD(24)
 A             MSGKEY                      SFLMSGKEY
 A             PSPGM                       SFLPGMQ
 *
 *-------------------------------------------------------------------
 * Error message subfile control record
 *-------------------------------------------------------------------
 A           R MSGCTL                      SFLCTL(MSGSFL)
 A                                         OVERLAY
 A N99                                     SFLDSP SFLDSPCTL SFLINZ SFLEND
 A                                         SFLSIZ(2) SFLPAG(1)
 A             PSPGM                       SFLPGMQ
```

Figure 13.4 Member MSGDS

```
... 1 ...+... 2 ...+... 3 ...+... 4 ...+... 5 ...+... 6 ...+... 7 ...+... 8
 *-------------------------------------------------------------------
 * MSGDS - Declares messaging-related variables and constants
 *
 * Function:
 *   Defines the MSGDTA data structure which declares several
 *   messaging-related variables and several messaging-related
 *   constants.
 *
 * MSGDTA - Messaging-related data structure variables:
 *    MSGID   - Message ID
 *    MSGF    - Message file
 *    MSGL    - Message library
 *     MSGFL     - Message file and library
 *    MSGTXT  - Message variable text
 *    MSGLEN  - Length of variable text
 *    MSGTYP  - Message type
 *    MSGQ    - Message queue
 *    MSGSTK  - Message stack
 *    MSGKEY  - Message key
 *    MSGNTY  - Message number type
 *    MSGPQ   - Message program queue
 *    MSGRMV  - Messages to remove
 *    MSGCNT  - Message count
 *
 * Messaging-related constants:
 *    MSBLK   - Blank
 *    MSNUL   - Null
 *    MSALL   - *ALL
 *    MSDIAG  - *DIAG
 *    MSESC   - *ESCAPE
 *    MSCSTK  - Current program stack  (0)
 *    MSPSTK  - Previous program stack (1)
 *    MSCURQ  - Current program queue  (*)
 *    MSLAST  - Last message sentinel text
```

Figure 13.4 Member MSGDS, continued

```
... 1 ...+... 2 ...+... 3 ...+... 4 ...+... 5 ...+... 6 ...+... 7 ...+... 8

     *    MSMAXM   - Maximum occurrences in ERRTBL data structure
     *----------------------------------------------------------------
IMSDDTA       IDS
I I              ' '                       1   7 MSGID
I I              ' '                       8  17 MSGF
I I              ' '                      18  27 MSGL
I                                          8  27 MSGFL
I I              ' '                      28 106 MSGTXT
I I              79                     B 107 1100MSGLEN
I I              ' '                      111 120 MSGTYP
I I              '*'                      121 130 MSGQ
I I              0                      B 131 1340MSGSTK
I I              ' '                      135 138 MSGKEY
I I              1                      B 157 1600MSGNTY
I I              '*'                      161 170 MSGPQ
I I              ' '                      171 180 MSGRMV
I I              0                        181 1900MSGCNT
     *
I                ' '             C            MSBLK
I                0               C            MSNUL
I                '*ALL'          C            MSALL
I                '*DIAG'         C            MSDIAG
I                '*ESCAPE'       C            MSESC
I                0               C            MSCSTK
I                1               C            MSPSTK
I                '*'             C            MSCURQ
I                '*LAST'         C            MSLAST
I                99              C            MSMAXM
```

Figure 13.5 Member MSGSND

```
... 1 ...+... 2 ...+... 3 ...+... 4 ...+... 5 ...+... 6 ...+... 7 ...+... 8

     *----------------------------------------------------------------
     * MSGSND - Send a message to a program message queue.
     *
     * Function:
     *   Send the message from a message file to a program message queue.
     *
     * Requires copy modules:
     *   ERRDS    - Error data structure
     *   MSGDS    - Messaging-related data structure
     *
     * Expects:
     *   MSGID    - Message ID
     *   MSGF     - Message file
     *   MSGL     - Message library
     *   MSGTXT   - Message replacement text (optional)
     *   MSGLEN   - Length of message replacement text (optional)
     *   MSGTYP   - Message type
     *   MSGQ     - Call message queue
     *   MSGSTK   - Call stack counter
```

Figure 13.5 Member MSGSND, continued

```
... 1 ...+... 2 ...+... 3 ...+... 4 ...+... 5 ...+... 6 ...+... 7 ...+... 8

 *    MSGKEY    - Message key (always blanks)
 *    ERRDS     - Error data structure
 *
 * Returns:
 *    ERRDS     - Standard API error data structure
 *
 *-------------------------------------------------------------------------
C           MSGSND     BEGSR
 *
C                       CALL 'QMHSNDPM'
C                       PARM            MSGID
C                       PARM            MSGFL
C                       PARM            MSGTXT
C                       PARM            MSGLEN
C                       PARM            MSGTYP
C                       PARM            MSGQ
C                       PARM            MSGSTK
C                       PARM            MSGKEY
C                       PARM            ERRDS
 *
C                       ENDSR
```

Figure 13.6 Member MSGCLR

```
... 1 ...+... 2 ...+... 3 ...+... 4 ...+... 5 ...+... 6 ...+... 7 ...+... 8

 *-------------------------------------------------------------------------
 * MSGCLR - Remove all messages from program message queue.
 *
 * Function:
 *    Extracts all messages from the current program's message queue.
 *
 * Requires copy modules:
 *    ERRDS     - Error data structure
 *    MSGDS     - Messaging-related data structure
 *
 * Expects:
 *    MSCURQ    - Messages from current queue
 *    MSCSTK    - Messages from current program
 *    MSALL     - Remove all messages
 *    ERRDS     - Error data structure
 *
 * Returns:
 *    ERRDS     - Standard API error data structure
 *
 *-------------------------------------------------------------------------
C           MSGCLR     BEGSR
 *
C                       MOVELMSCURQ     MSGQ      P
C                       MOVELMSCSTK     MSGSTK    P
C                       MOVE *BLANKS    MSGKEY
C                       MOVELMSALL      MSGRMV    P
```

Figure 13.6 Member MSGCLR, continued

```
... 1 ...+... 2 ...+... 3 ...+... 4 ...+... 5 ...+... 6 ...+... 7 ...+... 8
 *
C                       CALL  'QMHRMVPM'
C                       PARM            MSGQ
C                       PARM            MSGSTK
C                       PARM            MSGKEY
C                       PARM            MSGRMV
C                       PARM            ERRDS
 *
C                       ENDSR
```

Using Data Structures as Program Parameters

Chapter 14

Power-up the capability of called programs to "talk" to each other by using data structures as program parameters.

Using called RPG programs is an effective way to write modular, robust applications that are easy to maintain. At first glance, though, the capability appears a bit constrained because the types of parameters you can pass from program to program seem limited to simple program variables. This chapter debunks that myth and shows you how to add to RPG's program-call capabilities by using data structures as program parameters. Like several of the programs in this book, the programs presented in this chapter use some routines from previous chapters. Before we discuss using data structures as parameters, let's review RPG's method of passing parameters from one program to another.

In RPG, parameters are passed by reference — that is, the address of a parameter, not a parameter's actual value, is what is actually passed from program to program. Consider the following snippets:

```
 * Program A
C                        Z-ADD5          TSTVAL 150
C                        CALL PGMB                    99
C                        PARM            TSTVAL
 * TSTVAL now equal to 15 in Program A


 * Program B
C           *ENTRY       PLIST
C                        PARM TSTVAL
C                        ADD  10         TSTVAL
C                        RETRN
```

Before calling Program B, Program A sets the value of TSTVAL to 5. After the call to Program B, though, the value of TSTVAL in Program A is 15 — because Program B added 10 to TSTVAL. This change in the value of TSTVAL is reflected in Program A because the address of TSTVAL was passed to Program B — thus, any changes Program B made to the value stored at that address would be reflected in Program A (or any other program to which TSTVAL had been passed). It's important to realize that Program A didn't pass the value of field TSTVAL to Program B; Program A simply passed the address of field TSTVAL to Program B.

This concept of passing addresses rather than actual values is behind RPG's ability to pass multiple-occurrence data structures (MODS) from program to program — the actual data structure isn't passed, merely the *address* of the data structure. Using a multiple-occurrence data structure is an excellent way to pass a variable number of parameters between programs. We use them extensively with interactive work-with programs to pass lists of selected records (and associated data) to subprograms, but the technique has many other uses.

While it's not absolutely necessary, the first step we recommend you take when using multiple-occurrence data structures for program parameters is to create a /COPY member that describes the data structure you'll be using as a parameter. By using a /COPY member, you can be sure the multiple-occurrence data structure will be defined correctly and consistently in every program that references it. Figure 14.1 shows an example /COPY member. In this example, a 99-occurrence data structure is defined that will be used to pass customer information for up to 99 customers from one program to another. Each occurrence includes the customer's number, name, two telephone numbers, and the customer's account balance. The maximum number of occurrences you require will depend on your application. In this case, we assume that users typically won't attempt to select more than 99 customers to work with at once.

The member in Figure 14.1 also defines a constant and a field that programs need to reference this structure. The named constant CUMAX defines the maximum occurrence that can be stored in, or otherwise referenced in, the CUSINF data structure (this number cannot be determined dynamically in RPG). If you change the number of occurrences (in positions 44-47 of the first line of the data structure declaration) of the CUSINF data structure, you must also change the constant value of CUMAX accordingly (also, don't forget to recompile all programs that use the data structure's /COPY member). The field declared in this member, CUENTS, will be used to track the actual number of occurrences being referenced in the CUSINF data structure. By declaring the data structure, the named constant, and the one field in one /COPY member, you ensure that all RPG programs will automatically have access to the data they need to work with the CUSINF data structure.

Figure 14.1 /COPY Member with Multiple-Occurence Data Structure Definition

```
... 1 ...+... 2 ...+... 3 ...+... 4 ...+... 5 ...+... 6 ...+... 7 ...+... 8

  *
ICUSINF       DS                      99
I                                      1     70CUSNO
I                                      8   37 CUSNAM
I                                     38   52 CUSPH1
I                                     53   67 CUSPH2
I                                     67   772CUSBAL
  *
I             99                   C          CUMAX
  *
I             IDS
I                                      1   150CUENTS
```

Figure 14.2 shows the stub of an RPG program filling 24 occurrences of CUSINF and then passing that data structure to another RPG program. The CUSINF data structure can contain up to 99 occurrences and the CUENTS field is used to signal to the called program how many of them actually contain active data. Note that the CUSINF data structure and the CUENTS field are both passed to the called program. The called program will use CUENTS to determine how many of the 99 occurrences of CUSINF it should process.

Figure 14.2 Passing a Multiple-Occurrence Data Structure to a Program

```
... 1 ...+... 2 ...+... 3 ...+... 4 ...+... 5 ...+... 6 ...+... 7 ...+... 8

  /COPY CUSINF
  :
  :
  * Fill 24 DS entries with data
C             1         DO    24      X
C             X         OCCURCUSINF
C                       .. fill CUSINF structure here
C                       ENDDO
C                       Z-ADD24       CUENTS
  *
C                       CALL  'PGMA'
C                       PARM          CUSINF
C                       PARM          CUENTS
```

Figure 14.3 shows a stub of the program called from the stub shown in Figure 14.2. To ensure that the calling program doesn't misinform the called program, this stub provides a defensive test to ensure that the number of CUSINF entries to process doesn't exceed what the called program thinks is the maximum number of occurrences for CUSINF (based on the value of CUMAX). This test ensures that the calling program didn't put an inappropriate value in the CUENTS field. After ensuring that CUENTS is okay, the called program then reads the specified number of occurrences from the CUSINF data structure. In this example, each occurrence can be put in a subfile so a user can display data and further work with the customer data received.

Figure 14.3 Processing the Passed Data Structure

```
... 1 ...+... 2 ...+... 3 ...+... 4 ...+... 5 ...+... 6 ...+... 7 ...+... 8

 /COPY CUSINF
C           *ENTRY    PLIST
C                     PARM            CUSINF
C                     PARM            CUENTS
   :
 * Check for maximum entries exceeded.
C           CUENTS    IFGT CUMAX
   : Error processing here for maximum entries exceeded
C                     ENDIF
 *
 * Read each occurrence of the CUSINF passed.
C           1         DO   CUENTS    X
C           X         OCCURCUSINF
   :                      .. do something with an
   :                      .. occurrence of CUSINF here
C                     ENDDO
```

The technique presented in this chapter shows how to pass a specific multiple-occurrence data structure as a program parameter. While the examples are all specialized to work with the CUSINF data structure, you can easily create your own data structures to use as parameters. The technique of passing a multiple-occurrence data structure as a parameter has many interesting and useful purposes. You'll find that giving just a little thought to creating reusable routines to manage the process easily produces good results.

If you are skeptical of this technique because of performance implications, relax. Because an address is being passed rather than actual data, using a multiple-occurrence data structure — of any size — as a program parameter has no more performance impact than passing the address of a single integer value. Further, the technique is actually a memory-saving technique, because the actual data structure only exists in one program; other programs are simply accessing the already-existing data structure in that program.

Ending Interactive Programs Automatically

Chapter 15

Avoid potential security problems and annoying operational interruptions by ending unattended interactive programs automatically and gracefully.

You can have level 40 security active on your AS/400, change passwords frequently, and be diligent about managing object authorization; but even the simplest thing can render all this defensive security planning useless. For example, consider the payroll manager who walks away from a sensitive payroll application for what was to be just a few minutes — but ends up recounting a recent skiing trip in excruciating detail near the company coffee pot for 45 minutes. While the manager is telling her skiing story, the sensitive application she was using, not to mention her signed-on interactive session, are at the mercy of any prying eyes or fingertips that make their way to her empty desk.

Beyond security concerns, consider the interactive application that is accidentally left open overnight, keeping nighttime processing from acquiring exclusive use of database files for maintenance or purging. It's very annoying to arrive early in the morning to discover that nighttime processing didn't end normally because an active application interfered.

With just a little extra coding, you can avoid either of these scenarios by adding the logic to your RPG programs to cause them to end in a planned, graceful fashion. You can implement this technique with a little "swindle" using the DDS INVITE keyword, which is normally intended for use with multiple acquired devices attached to a display file. In this case, we're only using one device per program. The CRTDSPF's WAITRCD parameter, which specifies a time-out value, can be used to create a display file that will trigger a time-out event to which your RPG program can react.

To see the technique in action, compile the DDS shown in Figure 15.1 with the following command:

```
CRTDSPF FILE( library/dspf )        +
        SRCFILE( library/srcfile )  +
        WAITRCD( 15 )
```

The WAITRCD value specifies how long any one screen format in the resulting display file will be displayed before a time-out occurs. Within the DDS specifications, note the use of the file-level keyword INVITE. WAITRCD is only valid for read-from-invited-devices operations; thus, the INVITE keyword is necessary. Providing a WAITRCD value with the CRTDSPF command and having a file-level keyword are the only two display file special conditions for this technique.

The corresponding RPG program for the DDS in Figure 15.1 is shown in Figure 15.2. For the RPG program you want to time-out, you need to specify a file feedback data structure for the WORKSTN file and provide one F-specification continuation line. The file feedback data structure is specified with the WSDS member from Figure 5.1 (Chapter 5); its WSSTAT field provides the means to determine that a time-out has occurred. Specify the name of this file feedback structure, WSDS, following the INFDS keyword on the first line of the F-specification. The other F-specification continuation line provides the NUM keyword, which specifies the number of devices defined for the associated WORKSTN file. For screen time-out purposes, you'll always use 1 for this value (don't worry, your operators will be able to successfully use concurrent copies of this program). In addition to including the WSDS member, also include the WSCONS and WSCUA members from Chapter 5 (for the named constants they provide). Note also that while not absolutely necessary, this program includes the CTLWDMP, ERRDS, PGMSDS, and PSSR members for enhanced error-handling.

All that's necessary now is to provide your RPG program with what it needs to interpret and react to a time-out situation. To do this, immediately after each display file READ operation (be sure to specify an error indicator in columns 56-57), check the value of the WSSTAT field. If the value is 1331 (which is defined by the WSCONS member with the named constant WSTO), a time-out will have occurred (that is, the time you specified with the WAITRCD parameter has expired and control has been automatically returned to your program). You can use the WSSTAT field to condition any code necessary to end your program, or perhaps to cause it to redisplay the previously displayed format. Note that this technique *requires* the WRITE/READ combination; the EXFMT operation will not work.

The example RPG program in Figure 15.2 shows a way to track which screen format is currently displayed (using the CURSCR variable), and how you can vary what time-out action occurs for different formats. This program also uses one input/output parameter (TOEXIT), whose purpose is to convey to the calling program whether or not a time-out condition caused the program to end. If that was the case, you might want the CL that called this program to sign off the workstation, for security purposes. By calling QCMDEXC, you could even take such drastic measures from within the timed-out program, but you'll probably find that it is better to let the calling CL program manage any additional time-out action required.

Figure 15.1 DDS to Achieve Screen Time-Out

```
... 1 ...+... 2 ...+... 3 ...+... 4 ...+... 5 ...+... 6 ...+... 7 ...+... 8

 * DDS to achieve screen time-out.
 *
 * Use the following CRTDSPF command to create this display file.
 *
 * The WAITRCD parameter specifies, in seconds, the time the display
 * waits for input.
 *
 *     CRTDSPF FILE( library/dspf )          +
 *             SRCFILE( library/srcfile )    +
 *             WAITRCD( 15 )
 *
 *
A                                           DSPSIZ( 24 80 *DS3 )
A                                           PRINT
A                                           INVITE
 *-----------------------------------------------------------------
 * Input format SCREEN1
 *-----------------------------------------------------------------
A          R SCREEN1
A                                           CF03 CF12
 *
A                                       1 36'Screen #1'
A                                       4  8'Screen #1 input field.........'
A            WKNAME      24    B  4 40
A                                      15  2'Program automatically ends-
A                                            after 15 seconds of-
A                                            inactivity.'
A                                      23  2'F3=Exit'
A                                      23 11'F12=CANCEL'
 *-----------------------------------------------------------------
 * Input format SCREEN2
 *-----------------------------------------------------------------
A          R SCREEN2
A                                           CF03 CF12
 *
A                                       1 36'Screen #2'
A                                       4  8'Screen #2 input field.........'
A            WKNAME      24    B  4 40
A                                      15  2'Panel automatically ends-
A                                            after 15 seconds of-
A                                            inactivity.'
A                                      23  2'F3=Exit'
A                                      23 11'F12=CANCEL'
```

Figure 15.2 RPG Program Illustrating Screen Time-Out

```
... 1 ...+... 2 ...+... 3 ...+... 4 ...+... 5 ...+... 6 ...+... 7 ...+... 8

 /COPY CTLWDMP
FTIMEOUT CF  E                          WORKSTN      KINFDS WSDS
F                                                    KNUM          1
 /COPY ERRDS
 /COPY PGMSDS
 /COPY STDTYPES
 /COPY WSCONS
 /COPY WSCUA
 /COPY WSDS
 *
 *
C           *ENTRY    PLIST
C                     PARM            TOEXIT
 *   Stay in program until Exit or Cancel is pressed, or
 *   until SCREEN1 format times-out.
 *
 *
 * Assume TimeOutExit is false
C                     MOVEL*OFF       TOEXIT
 *
 * Set first screen to SCREEN1
C                     MOVEL'SCREEN1'  CURSCR  8 P
 *
C                     MOVEL*OFF       EXTPGM
C           EXTPGM    DOWEQ*OFF
 *
 * Read and write a screen
C                     EXSR WRTSCR
C                     READ TIMEOUT                      9899
 *
C                     SELEC
 * Handle EXIT keypress
C           WSKEY     WHEQ EXIT
C                     MOVEL*ON        EXTPGM
 *
 * Handle CANCEL keypress
C           WSKEY     WHEQ CANCEL
C                     MOVEL*ON        EXTPGM
 *
 * Handle screen time-out
C           WSSTAT    WHEQ WSTO
 * End program if current screen is SCREEN1
C           CURSCR    IFEQ 'SCREEN1'
C                     MOVEL*ON        TOEXIT
C                     MOVEL*ON        EXTPGM
C                     ENDIF
 *
C                     ENDSL
 *
 * Set next screen to display
C                     EXSR SETSCR
```

Figure 15.2 RPG Program Illustrating Screen Time-Out, Continued

```
... 1 ...+... 2 ...+... 3 ...+... 4 ...+... 5 ...+... 6 ...+... 7 ...+... 8
     *
C                      ENDDO
     *
C                      MOVEL*ON        *INLR
C                      RETRN
  *
  *
  *--------------------------------------------------------
  * WRTSCR - Write a screen
  *--------------------------------------------------------
C          WRTSCR     BEGSR
C                     SELEC
  * Display screen format based on CURSCR field
C          CURSCR     WHEQ 'SCREEN1'
C                     WRITESCREEN1
  *
C          CURSCR     WHEQ 'SCREEN2'
C                     WRITESCREEN2
C                     ENDSL
  *
C                     ENDSR
  *
  *
  *--------------------------------------------------------
  * SETSCR - Set next screen to display
  *--------------------------------------------------------
C          SETSCR     BEGSR
  *
C                     SELEC
  *
  * Follow SCREEN1 with SCREEN2
C          CURSCR     WHEQ 'SCREEN1'
C                     MOVEL'SCREEN2' CURSCR     P
  *
  * Follow SCREEN2 with SCREEN1
C          CURSCR     WHEQ 'SCREEN2'
C                     MOVEL'SCREEN1' CURSCR     P
C                     ENDSL
  *
C                     ENDSR
  *
  *
  *--------------------------------------------------------
  * *INZSR - Initialize program variables at start-up
  *--------------------------------------------------------
C          *INZSR     BEGSR
  * Define ExitProgram var
C          *LIKE      DEFN #BOOL     EXTPGM
  * Define TimeOutExit var
C          *LIKE      DEFN #BOOL     TOEXIT
  *
C                     ENDSR
  /COPY PSSR
```

Basic String Operations

Chapter 16

Although RPG/400 has acquired a few string operations over the years (e.g., SUBST and SCAN), its built-in string handling capabilities are still quite meager. This and the next three chapters provide RPG string-handling functions that substantially enhance RPG's built-in string capabilities.

As with most of the RPG code presented in this book, our string-handling routines are provided in a "building-block" style. By using these cut-and-paste routines, you can quickly and easily work with strings in your RPG programs. This chapter provides what we consider "basic" string operations. The string functions not only provide consistent feedback of errors but also avoid the factor cram associated with RPG's string operations. Our basic string operations include determining the logical length of a string, determining the length of a string with x trailing blanks added, determining the length of a string with trailing blanks removed, and converting the case of an entire string. Subsequent chapters provide more complex string operations (see Appendix B for an interactive program to test the 12 string functions presented in this and the following three chapters).

The first two members, STRDS and STDCONST, (Figures 16.1 and 16.2) from this chapter provide the data structures and named constants our string-handling routines require. Use the /COPY directive to include these two members somewhere in your program's I-specs for any program that uses our string-handling routines.

Member STRDS defines two string work fields, STR1 and STR2, which are each 256 characters long (the maximum-length RPG string field). Other numeric fields (e.g., string lengths, string positions, and string sizes) are also included in STRDS and associated with STR1 and STR2 to report the results of string operations (these fields all begin with STR, S1, or S2 prefixes). As you probably know, RPG doesn't support dynamically sized strings; rather, all strings are hard-coded to a given length. However, these string functions have been designed to mimic dynamically sized strings, using a 256-byte work field named STR1 to contain the results of the string functions. After using these string functions to modify the value in STR1, you can move that work field back into the target fields of your RPG programs.

Determining a Field's Logical Data Length

The STRLEN routine (Figure 16.3) returns the logical length of data in a string field up to the right-most, non-blank character in that string (see Chapter 20 for a technique to determine the physical length of any field). To use the STRLEN function, use the /COPY directive to include this function somewhere in the subroutine portion of your RPG program's C-specs. STRLEN requires that the STRDS and STDCONST members (provided earlier in this chapter) also be included.

STRLEN expects

- STR1 to contain the string for which the length is desired.

STRLEN returns

- STR1LN with the logical length of STR1 (i.e., if a field is defined as 12 characters long and contains the left-justified value "BOB," its logical length is 3).
- STRERR with the error condition.

Before calling STRLEN, use the MOVEL operation to move your target field into the STR1 work field. Don't forget to use the P op-code extender with the MOVEL operations when you move source values to STR1 or STR2. The P op-code extender forces the target field to blanks before the move is performed. If you forget the P op-code extender, it's possible to have left-over string contents remain in STR1, which would cause the string functions to return the wrong results.

All our string-handling routines use the STRERR field to report errors to the calling code — if an error occurs, STRERR will be set to 1; if not, STRERR will be set to 0. (Remember that 1 and 0 may also be represented by RPG's *ON and *OFF figurative constants, respectively). The STRLEN routine is a simple wrapper around RPG's CHEKR operation code, and STRLEN won't ever report an error. However, for syntactical consistency with our other string operations, the STRLEN function sets the STRERR field to *OFF — indicating an error did not occur when the STRLEN function was being executed.

For example, you could use the following code to determine the logical length of the data in the 32-byte TEXT field:

```
I/COPY STRDS
I/COPY STDCONST
    :
* Set source field to the value 'Test'
C                        MOVEL'Test'    TEXT    32 P
    :
C                        MOVELTEXT      STR1       P
C                        EXSR STRLEN
C                        Z-ADDSTR1LN    TEXTLN
```

After you use this code, the TEXTLN field contains the value 4. STRLEN isn't much value when used alone; but as you'll soon see, the information it provides about a string field can be used very effectively by our other string-handling routines.

Padding a String with Trailing Blanks

The STRPAD function (Figure 16.4) returns the length of a string padded with a specified number of trailing blanks. An error is returned if the source string length or the padded size is out of bounds (for example, an error occurs if you try to pad a 132-character string with 132 blanks because the padded string would be greater than the 256-byte string fields that RPG/400 provides). To use the STRPAD function, use the /COPY directive to include this function somewhere in the subroutine portion of your RPG program's C-specs. STRPAD requires that the STRDS and STDCONST members (provided earlier in this chapter) also be included.

STRPAD expects

- STR1 to contain the value of the string to pad.
- STR1LN to contain the logical length of STR1.
- STR1SZ to contain the number of blanks with which to pad STR1.

STRPAD returns

- STR1LN with the new logical length of the padded string.
- STRERR with error results.

Here is an example of using the STRPAD function to pad a salutation field with one trailing blank:

```
I/COPY STRDS
I/COPY STDCONST
        :
* Set source field to the value 'Ms.'
C                       MOVEL'Ms.'      SALUTE  8 P
        :
C                       MOVELSALUTE     STR1      P
C                       Z-ADD3          STR1LN
C                       Z-ADD1          STR1SZ
C                       EXSR STRPAD
C                       Z-ADDSTR1LN     PADLEN
```

The new logical padded length of STR1 is returned in STR1LN. As you can see, this example isn't too effective because the logical length of the salutation is hard-coded. However, the STRLEN function can be used to remove this hard-coded dependency:

```
I/COPY STRDS
I/COPY STDCONST
        :
* Set source field to the value 'Ms.'
C                       MOVEL'Ms.'      SALUTE  8 P
        :
C                       MOVELSALUTE     STR1      P
C                       EXSR STRLEN
C                       Z-ADD1          STR1SZ
C                       EXSR STRPAD
C                       Z-ADDSTR1LN     PADLEN
```

This code would now return the new length of the padded string, regardless of the logical length of the salutation field.

Trimming Trailing Blanks from a String

The STRTRM function (Figure 16.5) returns the length of a string with trailing blanks removed, up to a maximum string length. An error occurs if the string length is out of bounds or if the length of the trimmed string exceeds the specified maximum length. To use the STRTRM function, use the /COPY directive to include this function somewhere in the subroutine portion of your RPG program's C-specs. STRTRM requires that the STRDS and STDCONST members (provided earlier in this chapter) also be included.

STRTRM expects

- STR1 to contain the string value to trim.
- STR1LN to contain the maximum size for the trimmed string. If the length of the trimmed string exceeds this value, an error is returned.

STRTRM returns

- STR1LN with the length of the trimmed string.
- STRERR with error results.

The following example reports the trimmed length of the TEXT field, assuming a maximum trimmed value of 32:

```
I/COPY STRDS
I/COPY STDCONST
    :
C                       MOVELTEXT     STR1      P
C                       Z-ADD32       STR1LN
C                       EXSR STRTRM
C           STRERR      IFEQ *ON
C                       …trimmed string longer than maximum
C                       ELSE
C                       …OK to use STR1LN value
C                       END
```

Converting the Case of a String

The STRLWR and STRUPR functions (Figures 16.6 and 16.7) convert the case of a string to either lowercase or uppercase. Both functions work in a similar way, so this discussion focuses only on the STRLWR function. To use the STRLWR or STRUPR functions, use the /COPY directive to include them somewhere in the subroutine portion of your RPG program's C-specs. STRLWR and STRUPR require that the STRDS and STDCONST members (provided earlier in this chapter) also be included.

STRLWR expects

- STR1 to contain the string to convert to lowercase.

STRLWR returns

- STR1 with the input string converted to lowercase.
- STRERR with error results.

The following example converts the string TEXT to all lowercase:

```
I/COPY STRDS
I/COPY STDCONST
    :
C                       MOVELTEXT     STR1      P
C                       EXSR STRLWR
C                       MOVELSTR1     TEXT      P
```

Before it calls STRLWR, the source string TEXT is moved into the work field STR1; upon return from STRLWR, the converted source string is moved into the source field TEXT. Note that, like the STRLEN function, the STRLWR and STRUPR functions don't need to check for errors. Thus, they unconditionally return *OFF in the STRERR field for syntactical consistency with our other string functions.

Figure 16.1 STRDS RPG /COPY Member (Data Structures for String Functions)

```
... 1 ...+... 2 ...+... 3 ...+... 4 ...+... 5 ...+... 6 ...+... 7 ...+... 8

     *-------------------------------------------------------------
     * STRDS - Data structures for string functions
     *
     * Function:
     *   Defines data structures for String functions.
     *
     * STR1DS  - str1_DS:
     *   STR1   - str1_data
     *   STR1LN - str1_len
     *   STR1PS - str1_pos
     *   STR1SZ - str1_size
     *
     * STR2DS  - str2_DS:
     *   STR2   - str2_data
     *   STR2LN - str2_len
     *   STR2PS - str2_pos
     *   STR2SZ - str2_size
     *
     * STR3DS  - str3_DS:
     *   STR3   - str3_data
     *   STR3LN - str3_len
     *   STR3PS - str3_pos
     *   STR3SZ - str3_size
     *
     * STRVDS  - str_var_DS:
     *   STRP   - str_ptr
     *   STRERR - str_err
     *   STRSIZ - str_size
     *-------------------------------------------------------------
ISTR1DS      IDS
I                                       1 256 STR1
I                                     P 257 2580STR1LN
I                                     P 257 2580S1L
I                                     P 259 2600STR1PS
I                                     P 259 2600S1P
I                                     P 261 2620STR1SZ
I                                     P 261 2620S1S
     *
ISTR2DS      IDS
I                                       1 256 STR2
I                                     P 257 2580STR2LN
I                                     P 257 2580S2L
I                                     P 259 2600STR2PS
I                                     P 259 2600S2P
I                                     P 261 2620STR2SZ
I                                     P 261 2620S2S
     *
ISTR3DS      IDS
I                                       1 256 STR3
I                                     P 257 2580STR3LN
I                                     P 257 2580S3L
```

Figure 16.1 STRDS RPG /COPY Member (Data Structures for String Functions), continued

```
... 1 ...+... 2 ...+... 3 ...+... 4 ...+... 5 ...+... 6 ...+... 7 ...+... 8

I                                   P 259 2600STR3PS
I                                   P 259 2600S3P
I                                   P 261 2620STR3SZ
I                                   P 261 2620S3S
 *
ISTRVDS     IDS
I                                   P   1  20STRP
I                                         3  3 STRERR
I             256                   C        STRSIZ
 *
```

Figure 16.2 STDCONST RPG /COPY Member (Standard Named Constants)

```
... 1 ...+... 2 ...+... 3 ...+... 4 ...+... 5 ...+... 6 ...+... 7 ...+... 8

 *----------------------------------------------------------------
 * STDCONST - Standard named constants
 *
 * Function:
 *   Defines standard named constants for use in any program.
 *
 * Standard constants:
 *   BLK    - blank
 *   DGTC   - digit_chars
 *   DPC    - dec_pos_chars
 *   DPDGT  - dec_pos_digit
 *   DPMSK  - dec_pos_mask
 *   EOSTR  - end_of_string
 *   MINUS  - minus_sign
 *   PLUS   - plus_sign
 *   SGNC   - numeric_sign_chars
 *   UPRC   - upper_case_chars
 *   LWRC   - lower_case_chars
 *----------------------------------------------------------------
I              ' '                  C        BLK
I              '0123456789'         C        DGTC
I              '.'                  C        DPC
I              '9'                  C        DPDGT
I              .999999999           C        DPMSK
I              X'00'                C        EOSTR
I              '-'                  C        MINUS
I              '+'                  C        PLUS
I              '+-'                 C        SGNC
I              'ABCDEFGHIJKLMNOPQRST-C        UPRC
I              'UVWXYZ'
I              'abcdefghijklmnopqrst-C        LWRC
I              'uvwxyz'
 *
```

Figure 16.3 STRLEN RPG /COPY Member (Returns the Logical Length of a String)

```
... 1 ...+... 2 ...+... 3 ...+... 4 ...+... 5 ...+... 6 ...+... 7 ...+... 8

 *----------------------------------------------------------------
 * STRLEN - Length of string function
 *
 * Function:
 *   Returns the length of data in a string up to the last
 *   non-blank character.
 *
 * Requires copy modules:
 *   STRDS    - Data structure for string functions.
 *   STDCONST - Standard named constants.
 *
 * Expects:
 *   STR1     - String value for which to determine logical length
 *
 * Returns:
 *   STR1LN   - Logical length of STR1.
 *   STRERR   - Error indicator (always *OFF).
 *
 * Example:
 *   Find the length of the data in a string TEXT, and store
 *   the answer in TEXTLN.
 *
C*                     MOVELTEXT    STR1      P
C*                     EXSR STRLEN
C*                     Z-ADDSTR1LN  TEXTLN
 *----------------------------------------------------------------
C          STRLEN     BEGSR
 *
C                     MOVE *OFF     STRERR
 *
C          BLK        CHEKRSTR1     STR1LN
 *
C                     ENDSR
 *
```

Figure 16.4 STRPAD RPG /COPY Member (Returns the Length of a String Padded with
            ***x* Blanks)**

```
... 1 ...+... 2 ...+... 3 ...+... 4 ...+... 5 ...+... 6 ...+... 7 ...+... 8

 *----------------------------------------------------------------
 * STRPAD - Pad string with trailing blanks function
 *
 * Function:
 *   Returns the length of a string padded with x blanks, up to
 *   the specified size. Returns an error if string length or
 *   padded size is out of bounds.
 *
 * Requires copy modules:
 *   STRDS    - Data structure for string functions.
```

```
... 1 ...+... 2 ...+... 3 ...+... 4 ...+... 5 ...+... 6 ...+... 7 ...+... 8

     *    STDCONST - Standard named constants.
     *
     * Expects:
     *    STR1      - String to pad.
     *    STR1LN    - Logical size of STR1.
     *    STR1SZ    - Trailing blanks to add.
     *
     * Returns:
     *    STR1LN    - Length of STR1 with padded blanks.
     *    STRERR    - Error indicator.
     *
     * Example:
     *    Pad a string TEXT, of length TEXTLN, with one blank
     *    separator before concatenating another string.
     *
     *                     MOVELTEXT      STR1       P
    C*                     Z-ADDTEXTLN    STR1LN
    C*                     Z-ADD1         STR1SZ
    C*                     EXSR STRPAD
     *
    C*        STRERR       IFEQ *OFF
    C*                     MOVELSTR1      TEXT       P
    C*                     Z-ADDSTR1LN    TEXTLN
    C*                     ELSE
     *                     :
    C                      ENDIF
     *----------------------------------------------------------------
    C         STRPAD       BEGSR
     *
    C                      MOVE *OFF      STRERR
     *
     * Set new string length
     *
    C         STR1LN    ADD  STR1SZ       STRP
     *
     * Pad with trailing blanks when no errors
     *
    C                      SELEC
     *
    C         STRP      WHGT STRSIZ
    C         STR1LN    ORGT STRSIZ
    C         STR1SZ    ORGT STRSIZ
    C                      MOVE *ON       STRERR
     *
    C                      OTHER
    C                      Z-ADDSTRP      STR1LN
     *
    C                      ENDSL
     *
    C                      ENDSR
     *
```

Figure 16.5 STRTRM RPG /COPY Member (Trim Trailing Blanks from a String)

```
... 1 ...+... 2 ...+... 3 ...+... 4 ...+... 5 ...+... 6 ...+... 7 ...+... 8

     *------------------------------------------------------------
     * STRTRM - Trim trailing blanks from string function
     *
     * Function:
     *   Returns the length of a string with trailing blanks removed
     *
     * Requires copy modules:
     *   STRDS    - Data structure for string functions
     *   STDCONST - Standard named constants
     *
     * Expects:
     *   STR1     - String value to trim
     *   STR1LN   - Maximum length of trimmed string.
     *
     * Returns:
     *   STR1LN   - Length of trimmed string.
     *   STRERR   - Error indicator.
     *
     * Example:
     *   Return length of string TEXT with trailing blanks
     *   removed, with minimum length of TEXTLN.
     *
C*                    MOVELTEXT      STR1      P
C*                    Z-ADDTEXTLN    STR1LN
C*                    EXSR STRTRM
C*                    MOVELSTR1      TEXT      P
C*                    Z-ADDSTR1LN    TEXTLN
     *------------------------------------------------------------
C           STRTRM    BEGSR
     *
C                     MOVE *OFF      STRERR
     *
     * Set position of last non-blank
     *
C           BLK       CHEKRSTR1      STRP
     *
     * Trim trailing blanks when no errors
     *
C                     SELEC
     *
C           STR1LN    WHGT STRSIZ
C           STR1LN    ORLT STRP
C                     MOVE *ON       STRERR
     *
C                     OTHER
C                     Z-ADDSTRP      STR1LN
     *
C                     ENDSL
     *
C                     ENDSR
     *
```

Figure 16.6 STRLWR RPG /COPY Member (Convert a String to Lowercase)

```
... 1 ...+... 2 ...+... 3 ...+... 4 ...+... 5 ...+... 6 ...+... 7 ...+... 8


 *----------------------------------------------------------------
 * STRLWR - Convert string to lowercase function
 *
 * Function:
 *   Convert a string to lowercase characters.
 *
 * Requires copy modules:
 *   STRDS    - Data structure for string functions.
 *   STDCONST - Standard named constants.
 *
 * Expects:
 *   STR1     - String to convert to lowercase.
 *
 * Returns:
 *   STR1     - String converted to lowercase.
 *   STRERR   - Error indicator (always *OFF).
 *
 * Example:
 *   Convert a string TEXT to lowercase.
 *
C*                    MOVELTEXT     STR1       P
C*                    EXSR STRLWR
C*                    MOVELSTR1     TEXT       P
 *----------------------------------------------------------------
C          STRLWR     BEGSR
 *
C                     MOVE *OFF     STRERR
 *
 * Convert to lowercase
 *
C          UPRC:LWRC XLATESTR1      STR1
 *
C                     ENDSR
```

Figure 16.7 STRUPR RPG /COPY Member (Convert a String to Uppercase)

```
 ... 1 ...+... 2 ...+... 3 ...+... 4 ...+... 5 ...+... 6 ...+... 7 ...+... 8

     *-----------------------------------------------------------------
     * STRUPR - Convert string to uppercase function
     *
     * Function:
     *   Convert a string to uppercase characters.
     *
     * Requires copy modules:
     *   STRDS     - Data structure for string functions.
     *   STDCONST  - Standard named constants.
     *
     * Expects:
     *   STR1      - String to convert to uppercase.
     *
     * Returns:
     *   STR1      - String converted to uppercase.
     *   STRERR    - Error indicator (always *OFF).
     *
     * Example:
     *   Convert a string TEXT to uppercase.
     *
     C*                      MOVELTEXT    STR1      P
     C*                      EXSR STRUPR
     C*                      MOVELSTR1    TEXT      P
     *-----------------------------------------------------------------
     C          STRUPR    BEGSR
     *
     C                      MOVE *OFF     STRERR
     *
     * Convert to uppercase
     *
     C          LWRC:UPRC XLATESTR1      STR1
     *
     C                      ENDSR
```

Substring and String Concatenation Operations

Chapter 17

This chapter presents two useful string operations: string concatenation (the ability to join two strings together), and sub-stringing (the ability to extract a part of a string). While RPG offers the basic functionality of these operations with its SUBST and CAT operation codes, you'll find that these functions provide more robust error handling and a few extra features.

Extracting a Part of a String

The STRSUB routine (Figure 17.1) presents a robust alternative to RPG's SUBST operation code for performing substring operations. STRSUB provides built-in error trapping and lets you easily extract a substring value from a given location in the source string up to the end of the source string. To use the STRSUB function, use the /COPY directive to include this function somewhere in the subroutine portion of your RPG program's C-specs. STRSUB requires that the STRDS and STDCONST members, and the STRLEN function, also be included (see Chapter 16 for a discussion of these).

STRSUB expects

- STR1 to contain the source string from which you want to extract a substring.

- STR1PS to contain the starting position of the substring in STR1.

- STR1SZ to contain the size of substring desired. Setting STR1SZ to 256 causes the substring returned to start at the position specified and end at the logical end of the source string.

STRSUB returns

- STR1 with the extracted substring.

- STR1LN with the logical length of the extracted substring.

- STRERR with the error condition. An error is returned and the substring operation isn't performed if the substring starting position or substring size is out of bounds.

For example, to extract an 8-byte string from the TEXT field, starting at position 11, you would use the following code:

```
C                         MOVELTEXT       STR1       P
C                         Z-ADD11         STR1PS
C                         Z-ADD8          STR1SZ
C                         EXSR STRSUB
 *
C           STRERR        IFEQ *OFF
C                         MOVELSTR1       WORD       P
C                         Z-ADDSTR1LN     WORDLN
 * WORD now contains the extracted substring and WORDLN
 * contains the logical length of the substring.
C                         ELSE
C    :                    Error occurred
C                         ENDIF
```

To extract a substring beginning at position 5 and continuing to the end of the source string, you would use

```
I/COPY STRDS
I/COPY STDCONST
    :
C                         MOVELTEXT       STR1       P
C                         Z-ADD5          STR1PS
C                         Z-ADDSTRSIZ     STR1SZ
C                         EXSR STRSUB
```

In this example, if TEXT contained the value 'Love Potion #9', the value returned in STR1 would be 'Potion #9'. This example uses the STRSIZ named constant value to specify 256 as the size of the substring to return — which indicates to STRSUB to return a substring from the starting position to the end of the string. STRSIZ is defined in the STRDS member (shown in Chapter 16's Figure 16.1).

Concatenating Strings

The STRCAT function (Figure 17.2) concatenates, or joins, two string values. STRCAT is an alternative to RPG/400's CAT operation code; however, unlike CAT, STRCAT is able to include trailing blanks and detect truncation. CAT always excludes trailing blanks. To insert space separators between the strings being concatenated, you would use the STRPAD string function (presented in Chapter 16) in conjunction with the STRCAT function (this chapter ends with an example of this). To use the STRCAT function, use the /COPY directive to include this function somewhere in the subroutine portion of your RPG program's C-specs. STRCAT requires that the STRDS and STDCONST members, and the STRLEN function, also be included (see Chapter 16 for a discussion of these).

STRCAT expects

- STR1 to contain the first string to concatenate.
- STR1LN to contain the length of STR1. Setting STR1LN to 256 causes the logical length of STR1 to be used.

- STR2 to contain the second string to concatenate.
- STR2LN to contain the length of STR2. Setting STR2LN to 256 causes the logical length of STR2 to be used.

STRCAT returns

- STR1 with the concatenated string values.
- STR1LN with the logical length of the concatenated string.
- STRERR with the error condition. An error is returned if string truncation would occur during concatenation or if the length of the concatenated string would exceed 256.

For example, if the field WORD1 contains the value 'AS' and the field WORD2 contains the value '/400', the following code:

```
I/COPY STRDS
I/COPY STDCONST
    :
C                    MOVELWORD1      STR1      P
C                    Z-ADD2          STR1LN
C                    MOVELWORD2      STR2      P
C                    Z-ADD4          STR2LN
C                    EXSR STRCAT
```

would concatenate the two values, returning 'AS/400' in the STR1 field, and '6' in the STR1LN field (the logical length of STR1).

Let's take a look at an example that uses the STRPAD function from Chapter 16 with this chapter's STRCAT function. This use of STRPAD shows how to add separator spaces for string concatenation. This example concatenates a city/state/zipcode string from three separate field values.

```
I/COPY STRDS
I/COPY STDCONST
    :
I             'Indianapolis'     C         VCITY
I             'IN'               C         VSTATE
I             '46992'            C         VZIP
I             50                 C         CSZSIZ
    :
* Set source field values.
C                    MOVELVCITY      CITY    32 P
C                    MOVELVSTATE     STATE    2 P
C                    MOVELVZIP       ZIP     10 P
C                    MOVEL*BLANKS    CSZ     50
*
* Concatenate city name with a comma and trailing space.
C                    MOVELCITY       STR1       P
C                    Z-ADDSTRSIZ     STR1LN
C                    MOVEL', '       STR2       P
C                    Z-ADD2          STR2LN
C                    EXSR STRCAT
*
```

```
* Concatenate state with STR1.
C                      MOVELSTATE    STR2
C                      Z-ADDSTRSIZ   STR2LN
C                      EXSR STRCAT
*
* Pad STR1 with three trailing blanks.
C                      EXSR STRLEN
C                      Z-ADD3        STR1SZ
C                      EXSR STRPAD
*
* Concatenate zipcode with STR1.
C                      MOVELZIP      STR2
C                      Z-ADDSTRSIZ   STR2LN
C                      EXSR STRCAT
* STR1 now contains the left-justified value:
* Indianapolis, IN   46992
* and STR1LN contains 24, the logical length of
* concatenated value in STR1.
* Now, save the concatenated value in the
* field named CSZ.
C          STRERR      IFEQ *OFF
C                      MOVELSTR1     CSZ         P
C                      ELSE
    :                  Error occurred
C                      ENDIF
```

Note that, in this example, the CITY, STATE, and ZIP fields are all concatenated using string lengths of STRSIZ (which is a named constant for the value 256) to cause the logical length of these fields to be used for string concatenation. Using this feature of STRCAT makes it easy to perform concatenation without regard for the string lengths. Note also how the STRPAD function is used to append three blank spaces to the string after the state name has been concatenated. Using STRPAD here is what causes the three blanks to appear between the state and the zip code in the final concatenated result.

This example also illustrates how the STR1 value is used as a perpetual target for subsequent string operations. Knowing that the string functions used expect input in STR1 and return output in STR1, once it has set the initial value of STR1 (with the CITY field), this code simply uses the string functions to continually transform the value of STR1 until the desired results are achieved.

Figure 17.1 STRSUB RPG /COPY Member (Extract Substring Function)

```
... 1 ...+... 2 ...+... 3 ...+... 4 ...+... 5 ...+... 6 ...+... 7 ...+... 8


*-----------------------------------------------------------------
* STRSUB - Substring function
*
* Function:
*   Extract a substring of the specified position and size
*   from a string. Returns an error if position or size is
```

```
... 1 ...+... 2 ...+... 3 ...+... 4 ...+... 5 ...+... 6 ...+... 7 ...+... 8
  *    out of bounds.
  *
  * Requires copy modules:
  *    STRDS    - Data structure for string functions.
  *    STDCONST - Standard named constants.
  *    STRLEN   - Determine logical length of string.
  *
  * Expects:
  *    STR1   - String from which to extract a value.
  *    STR1PS - Starting position of substring in STR1.
  *    STR1SZ - Size of substring. If this value is 256
  *             (STRSIZ), then a substring starting at STR1PS
  *             up to the logical end of the string is returned.
  *
  * Returns:
  *    STR1   - Substring value.
  *    STR1LN - Substring length.
  *    STRERR - Error indicator. Returns an error if string position
  *             or string size is out of bounds.
  *
  * Example:
  *    Extract a WORD from a string TEXT, of length TEXTLN,
  *    of 8 characters starting in position 11.
  *
C*                      MOVELTEXT    STR1       P
C*                      Z-ADD11      STR1PS
C*                      Z-ADD8       STR1SZ
C*                      EXSR STRSUB
  *
C*          STRERR      IFEQ *OFF
C*                      MOVELSTR1    WORD       P
C*                      Z-ADDSTR1LN  WORDLN
C*                      ELSE
  *                     :
C                       ENDIF
  *-----------------------------------------------------------------
C           STRSUB      BEGSR
  *
C                       MOVE *OFF    STRERR
  *
  * Set substring length if requested to end of string
  *
C           STR1SZ      IFEQ STRSIZ
C                       EXSR STRLEN
C           STR1LN      SUB  STR1PS  STR1SZ
C                       ADD  1       STR1SZ
C                       END
  *
  * Set substring end position
  *
C           STR1PS      ADD  STR1SZ  STRP
C                       SUB  1       STRP
```

Figure 17.1 STRSUB RPG /COPY Member (Extract Substring Function), continued

```
 ... 1 ...+... 2 ...+... 3 ...+... 4 ...+... 5 ...+... 6 ...+... 7 ...+... 8

     *
     * Substring when no errors
     *
   C                     SELEC
     *
   C          STR1PS     WHLT 1
   C          STR1PS     ORGT STRSIZ
   C          STR1SZ     ORGT STRSIZ
   C          STRP       ORGT STRSIZ
   C                     MOVE *ON        STRERR
     *
   C                     OTHER
   C                     Z-ADDSTR1SZ     STR1LN
   C                     Z-ADDSTR1PS     STRP
   C          STR1SZ     SUBSTSTR1:STRP STR1      P
     *
   C                     ENDSL
     *
   C                     ENDSR
```

Figure 17.2 STRCAT RPG /COPY Member (Concatenate Strings Function)

```
 ... 1 ...+... 2 ...+... 3 ...+... 4 ...+... 5 ...+... 6 ...+... 7 ...+... 8

     *----------------------------------------------------------------
     * STRCAT - Concatenate strings function
     *
     * Function:
     *   Concatenates one string to the end of another string.
     *   To insert separator characters at the end of the first
     *   string, use the Pad String function STRPAD before
     *   concatenating the strings. Returns an error on truncation.
     *
     * Requires copy modules:
     *   STRDS    - Data structure for string functions
     *   STDCONST - Standard named constants
     *   STRLEN  - Determine logical length of string.
     *
     * Expects:
     *   STR1   - First string to concatenate.
     *   STR1LN - Length of STR1. Using STRSIZ (256) causes the logical
     *            length of STR1 to be used.
     *   STR2   - Second string to concatenate.
     *   STR2LN - Length of STR2. Using STRSIZ (256) causes the logical
     *            length of STR2 to be used.
     *
     * Returns:
     *   STR1   - Concatenated string.
     *   STR1LN - Length of concatenated string.
     *   STRERR - Error indicator. Returns an error if string truncation occurs
```

```
 ... 1 ...+... 2 ...+... 3 ...+... 4 ...+... 5 ...+... 6 ...+... 7 ...+... 8

 *              or if length of concatenated string would exceed 256.
 *
 * Example:
 *   Concatenate a WORD, of length WORDLN, to the end of a
 *   string TEXT, of length TEXTLN. To insert separator
 *   characters between TEXT and WORD, use the STRPAD function
 *   to pad TEXT with trailing blanks before concatenating
 *   WORD.
 *
C*                    MOVELTEXT      STR1      P
C*                    Z-ADDTEXTLN    STR1LN
C*                    MOVELWORD      STR2      P
C*                    Z-ADDWORDLN    STR2LN
C*                    EXSR STRCAT
 *
C*        STRERR      IFEQ *OFF
C*                    MOVELSTR1      TEXT      P
C*                    Z-ADDSTR1LN    TEXTLN
C*                    ELSE
 *                    ...
C*                    ENDIF
 *-----------------------------------------------------------------
C         STRCAT      BEGSR
 *
C                     MOVE *OFF      STRERR
 *
 * Use logical length of STR2?
 *
C         STR2LN      IFEQ STRSIZ
 * Save STR1 and STR1LN
C                     MOVELSTR1      STR3      P
C                     Z-ADDSTR1LN    STR3LN
 * Determine logical length of STR2
C                     MOVELSTR2      STR1      P
C                     EXSR STRLEN
 * Save length of STR2
C                     Z-ADDSTR1LN    STR2LN
 * Restore STR1 and STR1LN
C                     MOVELSTR3      STR1      P
C                     Z-ADDSTR3LN    STR1LN
C                     ENDIF
 *
 * Use logical length of STR1?
 *
C         STR1LN      IFEQ STRSIZ
C                     EXSR STRLEN
C                     ENDIF
 *
 * Set size of string
 *
C         BLK         CHEKRSTR1      STR1SZ
 *
```

```
... 1 ...+... 2 ...+... 3 ...+... 4 ...+... 5 ...+... 6 ...+... 7 ...+... 8

     * Set separator chars and length
     *
C             STR1LN    SUB  STR1SZ    STRP
C                       ADD  STR2LN    STR1LN
     *
     * Concatenate strings when no errors
     *
C                       SELEC
     *
C             STRP      WHLT 0
C             STR1LN    ORGT STRSIZ
C             STR2LN    ORGT STRSIZ
C                       MOVE *ON       STRERR
     *
C                       OTHER
C                       CAT  STR2:STRP STR1
     *
C                       ENDSL
     *
C                       ENDSR
```

Justifying and Centering Strings

Chapter 18

This chapter provides three string functions for justifying string values. With these functions, which have no direct RPG/400 alternative, you can left- or right-justify a string and you can center a string.

Right-Justifying a String

The STRRAJ function (Figure 18.1) right-justifies a string field. To use the STRRAJ function, use the /COPY directive to include this function somewhere in the subroutine portion of your RPG program's C-specs. STRRAJ requires that the STRDS and STDCONST members (see Chapter 16) also be included.

STRRAJ expects

- STR1 to contain the string value to right-justify.
- STR1SZ to contain the target length of the right-justified string.

STRRAJ returns

- STR1 with the string right-justified.
- STR1LN with the logical length of the justified string.
- STRERR with the error condition. An error is returned if the string length or adjusted size is out of bounds.

For example, to right-justify the string TEXT within a string size of 80 characters, you would use the following:

```
I/COPY STRDS
I/COPY STDCONST
     :
C                    MOVELTEXT      STR1      P
C                    Z-ADD80        STR1SZ
C                    EXSR STRRAJ
 *
C          STRERR    IFEQ *OFF
C                    MOVELSTR1      TEXT      P
C                    Z-ADDSTR1LN    TEXTLN
C                    ELSE
     :                Error occurred
C                    ENDIF
```

Left-Justifying a String

The STRLAJ function (Figure 18.2) left-justifies a string field. To use the STRLAJ function, use the /COPY directive to include this function somewhere in the subroutine portion of your RPG program's C-specs. STRLAJ requires that the STRDS and STDCONST members also be included (see Chapter 16).

STRLAJ expects

- STR1 to contain the string value to left-justify.
- STR1LN to contain the logical length of the source string (STR1) to justify.

STRLAJ returns

- STR1 with the string left-justified.
- STR1LN with the logical length of the justified string.
- STRERR with the error condition. An error is returned if the source string length is out of bounds.

For example, to left-justify the 40-character string TEXT, you would use the following:

```
I/COPY STRDS
I/COPY STDCONST
     :
C                      MOVELTEXT    STR1       P
C                      Z-ADD40      STR1LN
C                      EXSR STRLAJ
  *
C          STRERR      IFEQ *OFF
C                      MOVELSTR1    TEXT       P
C                      ELSE
     :                 Error occurred
C                      ENDIF
```

If you were unsure of the logical length of the source string you needed to left-justify, you could first call the STRLEN function (shown in Chapter 16's Figure 16.3). For example,

```
I/COPY STRDS
I/COPY STDCONST
     :
C                      MOVELTEXT    STR1       P
C                      EXSR STRLEN
C                      EXSR STRLAJ
```

Centering a String

The STRCTR function (Figure 18.3) centers a string field. This function is handy for centering report and screen headings when they are passed as parameters to programs. To use the STRCTR function, use the /COPY directive to include this function somewhere in the subroutine portion of your RPG program's C-specs. STRCTR requires that the STRDS and STDCONST members also be included (see Chapter 16).

STRCTR expects

- STR1 to contain the string to center.
- STR1LN to contain the logical length of the string to center (the logical length of STR1).
- STR1SZ to contain the centered string size.

STRCTR returns

- STR1 with the centered string.
- STR1LN with the length of the centered string (the value specified for the STR1SZ parameter).
- STRERR with the error condition. An error is returned if the string length or centered size is out of bounds.

For example, to center a report heading in the string HDG, of length 80, with a target centered size of 80 characters, you would use this code:

```
C                         MOVELHDG       STR1        P
C                         Z-ADD80        STR1LN
C                         Z-ADD80        STR1SZ
C                         EXSR STRCTR
 *
C            STRERR       IFEQ *OFF
C                         MOVELSTR1      HDG         P
C                         Z-ADDSTR1LN    HDGLN
C                         ELSE
C       :                ...
C                         ENDIF
```

Figure 18.1 STRRAJ RPG /COPY Member (Right-Adjust a String)

```
... 1 ...+... 2 ...+... 3 ...+... 4 ...+... 5 ...+... 6 ...+... 7 ...+... 8


*---------------------------------------------------------------
* STRRAJ - Right-justify string function
*
* Function:
*   Right-justifies the data in a string within a specified
*   size. Returns an error if string length or adjusted size
*   is out of bounds.
*
* Requires copy modules:
*   STRDS    - Data structure for string functions
*   STDCONST - Standard named constants
*
* Expects:
*   STR1   - the string value to right-justify.
*   STR1SZ - the target length of the right-justified string.
```

```
      *
      * Returns:
      *   STR1   - the string right-justified.
      *   STR1LN - the logical length of the justified string.
      *   STRERR - the error condition. An error is returned if the string
      *            length or adjusted size is out of bounds.
      *
      * Example:
      *   Right-justify the string TEXT within a string size of
      *   80 characters.
      *
     C*                     MOVELTEXT       STR1         P
     C*                     Z-ADD80         STR1SZ
     C*                     EXSR STRRAJ
      *
     C*          STRERR     IFEQ *OFF
     C*                     MOVELSTR1       TEXT         P
     C*                     Z-ADDSTR1LN     TEXTLN
     C*                     ELSE
      *                     ...
     C*                     ENDIF
      *-------------------------------------------------------------
     C           STRRAJ     BEGSR
      *
     C                      MOVE *OFF        STRERR
      *
      * Set position of last non-blank
      *
     C           BLK        CHEKRSTR1        STRP
      *
      * Pad with leading blanks when no errors
      *
     C                      SELEC
      *
     C           STRP       WHGT STR1SZ
     C           STR1SZ     ORGT STRSIZ
     C                      MOVE *ON         STRERR
      *
     C                      OTHER
     C                      Z-ADDSTR1SZ      STR1LN
     C           STR1SZ     SUB  STRP        STRP
     C                      MOVE *BLANKS     STR2
     C           STR2       CAT  STR1:STRP   STR1
      *
     C                      ENDSL
      *
     C                      ENDSR
```

Figure 18.2 STRLAJ RPG /COPY Member (Left-Adjust a String)

```
... 1 ...+... 2 ...+... 3 ...+... 4 ...+... 5 ...+... 6 ...+... 7 ...+... 8

    *----------------------------------------------------------------
    * STRLAJ - Left-adjust string function
    *
    * Function:
    *   Left-justifies the data in a string. Returns an error if
    *   string length is out of bounds.
    *
    * Requires copy modules:
    *   STRDS    - Data structure for string functions
    *   STDCONST - Standard named constants
    *
    * Expects:
    *   STR1    - the string value to left-justify.
    *   STR1LN  - the logical length of the source string (STR1) to justify.
    *
    * Returns:
    *   STR1    - the string left-justified.
    *   STR1LN  - the logical length of the justified string.
    *   STRERR  - the error condition. An error is returned if the source
    *             string length is out of bounds.
    *
    * Example:
    *   Left-justify the data in a string TEXT, of length TEXTLN.
    *
C*                      MOVELTEXT     STR1     P
C*                      Z-ADDTEXTLN   STR1LN
C*                      EXSR STRLAJ
    *
C*        STRERR        IFEQ *OFF
C*                      MOVELSTR1     TEXT     P
C*                      ELSE
    *                   ...
C*                      ENDIF
    *
    *----------------------------------------------------------------
C         STRLAJ        BEGSR
    *
C                       MOVE *OFF     STRERR
    *
    * Set position of first non-blank
    *
C         BLK           CHECKSTR1     STRP
    *
    * Trim leading blanks when no errors
    *
C                       SELEC
    *
C         STR1LN        WHGT STRSIZ
C         STR1LN        ORLT STRP
```

Figure 18.2 STRLAJ RPG /COPY Member (Left-Adjust a String), continued

```
 ... 1 ...+... 2 ...+... 3 ...+... 4 ...+... 5 ...+... 6 ...+... 7 ...+... 8

C                    MOVE *ON      STRERR
 *
 * Trimming is only necessary when there are leading
 * blanks (i.e.- when STRP is greater than 1)
 *
C          STRP      WHGT 1
C          STR1LN    SUB  STRP     STR1SZ
C                    ADD  1        STR1SZ
C          STR1SZ    SUBSTSTR1:STRP STR1      P
C                    Z-ADDSTR1SZ   STR1LN
 *
C                    ENDSL
 *
C                    ENDSR
```

Figure 18.3 STRCTR RPG /COPY Member (Center a String)

```
 ... 1 ...+... 2 ...+... 3 ...+... 4 ...+... 5 ...+... 6 ...+... 7 ...+... 8

 *----------------------------------------------------------------
 * STRCTR - Center string function
 *
 * Function:
 *   Center the data in a string within a specified size.
 *   Returns an error if string length or centered size is out
 *   of bounds.
 *
 * Requires copy modules:
 *   STRDS    - Data structure for string functions
 *   STDCONST - Standard named constants
 *
 * Expects:
 *   STR1   - the string to center.
 *   STR1LN - the logical length of the string to center
 *            (the logical length of STR1).
 *   STR1SZ - the centered string size.
 *
 * Returns:
 *   STR1   - the centered string.
 *   STR1LN - the length of the centered string (the value
 *            specified for the STR1SZ parameter)
 *   STRERR - the error condition. An error is returned if the
 *            string length or centered size is out of bounds.
 *
 * Example:
 *   Center a heading in the string HDG, of length HDGLN,
 *   within a string size of 80 characters.
 *
C*                   MOVELHDG      STR1      P
C*                   Z-ADDHDGLN    STR1LN
C*                   Z-ADD80       STR1SZ
```

Figure 18.3 STRCTR RPG /COPY Member (Center a String), continued

```
... 1 ...+... 2 ...+... 3 ...+... 4 ...+... 5 ...+... 6 ...+... 7 ...+... 8

C*                  EXSR STRCTR
 *
C*        STRERR    IFEQ *OFF
C*                  MOVELSTR1      HDG        P
C*                  Z-ADDSTR1LN    HDGLN
C*                  ELSE
 *                  ...
C*                  ENDIF
 *
 *-----------------------------------------------------------------
C         STRCTR    BEGSR
 *
C                   MOVE *OFF      STRERR
 *
 * Set position of first non-blank
 *
C         BLK       CHECKSTR1      STRP
 *
 * Trim leading blanks when no errors
 *
C                   SELEC
 *
C         STR1LN    WHGT STRSIZ
C         STR1SZ    ORGT STRSIZ
C         STRP      ORGT STR1LN
C                   MOVE *ON       STRERR
 *
C         STRP      WHGT 1
C                   SUB  STRP      STR1LN
C                   ADD  1         STR1LN
C         STR1LN    SUBSTSTR1:STRP STR1       P
 *
C                   ENDSL
 *
 * Center string when no error
 *
C         STRERR    IFEQ *OFF
C                   Z-ADDSTR1SZ    STR1LN
C         BLK       CHEKRSTR1      STRP
C         STR1SZ    SUB  STRP      STRP
C                   DIV  2         STRP
C                   MOVE *BLANKS   STR2
C         STR2      CAT  STR1:STRP STR1
C                   ENDIF
 *
C                   ENDSR
```

Searching Strings

Chapter 19

RPG/400 provides a rudimentary string-searching function with its SCAN operation code. This chapter's string functions put robust, easy-to-use wrappers around SCAN. With these functions, you can easily search a string to find occurrences of a specified string value, starting from either the left or the right side of the searched string.

Finding Left-Most Occurrences of a String Value

The STRFND function (Figure 19.1) finds the first occurrence (and, optionally, subsequent occurrences) of a specified value from the left side of a searched string. To use the STRFND function, use the /COPY directive to include this function somewhere in the subroutine portion of your RPG program's C-specs. STRFND requires that the STRDS and STRCONST members also be included (see Chapter 16).

STRFND expects

- STR1 to contain the string value to search.
- STR1LN to contain the length of the string value to search.
- STR1PS to contain the starting position of search.
- STR2 to contain the string value to search for.
- STR2LN to contain the length of the value to search for.

STRFND returns

- STR1PS with the position of the located search value.
- STRERR with the error condition. An error is returned if the search value is not found.

For example, if the 80-character field TEXT contained the value 'The quick red fox', the following code would locate the first occurrence of 'fox' in that string and put its location in the field WRDPS:

```
I/COPY STRDS
I/COPY STDCONST
   :
C                    MOVELTEXT      STR1           P
C                    Z-ADD80        STR1LN
C                    Z-ADD1         STR1PS
C                    MOVEL'fox'     STR2           P
C                    Z-ADD3         STR2LN
C                    EXSR STRFND
 *
C          STRERR    IFEQ *OFF
C                    Z-ADDSTR1PS    WRDPS
 * WRDPS now contains the value 15.
C                    ELSE
   :                 Search value wasn't found.
C                    ENDIF
```

Be careful how you specify search values when you use STRFND.
For example, consider the field TEXT with the string value 'this is a test'
and the need to find the first occurrence of the word 'is' in that field. At a
glance, you might think the following code returns the value 6:

```
C                    MOVELTEXT      STR1           P
C                    Z-ADD80        STR1LN
C                    Z-ADD1         STR1PS
C                    MOVEL'is'      STR2           P
C                    Z-ADD2         STR2LN
C                    EXSR STRFND
```

However, after this code is performed, STR2LN doesn't contain the
value 6; it contains the value 3 because it found the occurrence of 'is' in
the word 'This'. To avoid this problem, the search should have been
specified as

```
C                    MOVELTEXT      STR1           P
C                    Z-ADD80        STR1LN
C                    Z-ADD1         STR1PS
C                    MOVEL' is'     STR2           P
C                    Z-ADD3         STR2LN
C                    EXSR STRFND
```

Note the leading blank that was added to the search value (STR2);
also note that the search length (STR2LN) has been set to 3. This code
returns the expected search results of 5.

Using a DOWHILE loop and incrementing the search position
(STR1PS) each time a value is found, it's easy to iterate a string search
across an entire string. For example, given the value 'This is a test is a
test is a test is a test is a test', the following code locates each occurrence
of ' is' in that string:

```
I/COPY STRDS
I/COPY STDCONST
   :
I               'This is a test is -  C          VTEXT
I               'a test is a test i-
I               's a test is a test'
 *
C                       MOVELVTEXT      STR1        P
C                       EXSR STRLEN
C                       Z-ADD1          STR1PS
 *
C                       MOVEL' is'      STR2
C                       Z-ADD3          STR2LN
 *
 * Attempt to find first occurrence of ' is'
C                       EXSR STRFND
 *
C            STRERR     DOWNE*ON
   :
   : STR1PS now contains the location of an occurrence of ' is'
   :
   :                    Perform some code
   :
 * Bump search position to position immediately after
 * previous position found.
C                       ADD  1          STR1PS
 * Attempt search again.
C                       EXSR STRFND
C                       ENDDO
```

Finding Right-Most Occurrences of a String Value

The STRFNL function (Figure 19.2) finds the first occurrence (and, optionally, subsequent occurrences) of a specified value from the right side of a searched string. You'll probably use STRFND to find occurrences from the beginning of the string; but for those times when you need to search a string from end to beginning, STRFNL will come in handy. To use the STRFNL function, use the /COPY directive to include this function somewhere in the subroutine portion of your RPG program's C-specs. STRFND requires that the STRDS and STDCONST members (see Chapter 16), and the STRFNL function (provided earlier in this chapter) also be included.

STRFNL expects

- STR1 to contain the string value to search.
- STR1LN to contain the length of the string value to search.
- STR1PS to contain the right-most position at which the search ended.
- STR2 to contain the value to search for.
- STR2LN to contain the length of the value to search for.

STRFNL returns

- STR1PS with the position of the located search value.
- STRERR with the error condition. An error is returned if the search value is not found.

For example, given the value 'This is a test is a test is a test is a test', the following code locates the last occurrence of ' is' in that string:

```
I/COPY STRDS
I/COPY STDCONST
    :
I               'This is a test is -  C          VTEXT
I               'a test is a test i-
I               's a test is a test'
  *
C                  MOVELVTEXT      STR1       P
C                  EXSR STRLEN
C                  Z-ADDSTR1LN     STR1PS
  *
C                  MOVEL' is'      STR2
C                  Z-ADD3          STR2LN
C                  EXSR STRFNL
  *
C         STRERR   IFEQ *OFF
C                  Z-ADDSTR1PS     WRDPS
  * WRDPS now contains the value 45.
C                  ELSE
    :              Search value wasn't found.
C                  ENDIF
```

Note the use of the STRLEN function (from Chapter 16's Figure 16.3) to dynamically determine the length of the string being searched. To ensure that the last occurrence of ' is' is found, that same value is also used as the position at which to end the search. Had the value of STR1PS been set to anything less than 45 (ending the search just before the last occurrence of ' is'), STRFNL would have returned 35, the location of the next-to-the-last occurrence of ' is' in the searched string.

Figure 19.1 STRFND RPG /COPY Member (Find First Occurrence of a String)

```
... 1 ...+... 2 ...+... 3 ...+... 4 ...+... 5 ...+... 6 ...+... 7 ...+... 8


 *-------------------------------------------------------------
 * STRFND - Find first occurrence of string function
 *
 * Function:
 *   Finds the first occurrence of argument in a string,
 *   starting at the specified position.
 *
 * Requires copy modules:
 *   STRDS    - Data structure for string functions
 *   STDCONST - Standard named constants
```

Figure 19.1 STRFND RPG /COPY Member (Find First Occurrence of a String), continued

```
... 1 ...+... 2 ...+... 3 ...+... 4 ...+... 5 ...+... 6 ...+... 7 ...+... 8

       *
       * Expects:
       *   STR1   - String value to search.
       *   STR1LN - Length of string value to search.
       *   STR1PS - Starting position of search.
       *   STR2   - Value to search for.
       *   STR2LN - Length of value to search for.
       *
       * Returns:
       *   STR1PS - Position of search value.
       *   STRERR - Error indicator.
       *
       * Example:
       *   Find the first occurrence of "The" in a string TEXT, of
       *   length TEXTLN and store the position of the match in WRDPS.
       *
C*                      MOVELTEXT      STR1      P
C*                      Z-ADDTEXTLN    STR1LN
C*                      Z-ADD1         STR1PS
C*                      MOVEL'The'     STR2      P
C*                      Z-ADD3         STR2LN
C*                      EXSR STRFND
       *
C*           STRERR     IFEQ *OFF
C*                      Z-ADDSTR1PS    WRDPS
C*                      ELSE
       *                ...
C*                      ENDIF
       *----------------------------------------------------------------
C            STRFND     BEGSR
       *
C                       MOVE *OFF      STRERR
       *
       *  Set end position of shortest possible search result
       *
C            STR2LN     ADD  STR1PS    STRP
C                       SUB  1         STRP
       *
       * Find string when no errors
       *
C                       SELEC
       *
C            STR1PS     WHLT 1
C            STR1PS     ORGT STR1LN
C            STR1LN     ORGT STRSIZ
C            STR2LN     ORLT 1
C            STR2LN     ORGT STRSIZ
C            STRP       ORGT STRSIZ
C                       MOVE *ON       STRERR
       *
C                       OTHER
```

Figure 19.1 STRFND RPG /COPY Member (Find First Occurrence of a String), continued

```
... 1 ...+... 2 ...+... 3 ...+... 4 ...+... 5 ...+... 6 ...+... 7 ...+... 8

C              STR2:S2L   SCAN STR1:S1P   STRP
C                         Z-ADDSTRP       STR1PS
C              STRP       ADD  STR2LN      STRP
C                         SUB  1           STRP
C              STR1PS     IFEQ 0
C              STRP       ORGT STR1LN
C                         MOVE *ON         STRERR
C                         ENDIF
 *
C                         ENDSL
 *
C                         ENDSR
 *
```

Figure 19.2 STRFNL RPG /COPY Member (Find Last Occurrence of a String)

```
... 1 ...+... 2 ...+... 3 ...+... 4 ...+... 5 ...+... 6 ...+... 7 ...+... 8

 *-------------------------------------------------------------
 * STRFNL - Find last occurrence of string function
 *
 * Function:
 *    Finds the last occurrence of argument in a string,
 *    ending at the specified position.
 *
 * Requires copy modules:
 *    STRDS    - Data structure for string functions
 *    STDCONST - Standard named constants
 *    STRFND   - Find first occurrence of string function
 *
 * Expects:
 *    STR1   - String value to search.
 *    STR1LN - Length of string value to search.
 *    STR1PS - Position at which to end search.
 *    STR2   - Value to search for.
 *    STR2LN - Length of value to search for.
 *
 * Returns:
 *    STR1PS - Position of search value.
 *    STRERR - Error indicator.
 *
 * Example:
 *    Find the last occurrence of "The" in a string TEXT, of
 *    length TEXTLN and store the position of the match in WRDPS.
 *
C*                        MOVELTEXT        STR1       P
C*                        Z-ADDTEXTLN      STR1LN
C*                        Z-ADDTEXTLN      STR1PS
C*                        MOVEL'The'       STR2       P
C*                        Z-ADD3           STR2LN
C*                        EXSR STRFNL
```

Figure 19.2 STRFNL RPG /COPY Member (Find Last Occurrence of a String), continued

```
... 1 ...+... 2 ...+... 3 ...+... 4 ...+... 5 ...+... 6 ...+... 7 ...+... 8
     *
C*          STRERR    IFEQ *OFF
C*                    Z-ADDSTR1PS    WRDPS
C*                    ELSE
     *                :
C*                    ENDIF
     *
     *----------------------------------------------------------------
C           STRFNL    BEGSR
     *
C           *LIKE     DEFN STR1PS    @FLSLP
C           *LIKE     DEFN STR1PS    @FLSSP
     *
C                     MOVE *OFF      STRERR
     *
     * Find string while no errors
     *
C                     Z-ADD0         @FLSSP
C                     Z-ADDSTR1PS    @FLSLP
C                     Z-ADD1         STR1PS
C                     EXSR STRFND
     *
C           STRERR    DOWEQ*OFF
C           STR1PS    ANDLE@FLSLP
C*
C                     Z-ADDSTR1PS    @FLSSP
C                     ADD  1         STR1PS
C                     EXSR STRFND
     *
C                     ENDDO
     *
     * Search ok if string found before end position
     *
C           @FLSSP    IFGT 0
C           @FLSSP    ANDLE@FLSLP
C                     Z-ADD@FLSSP    STR1PS
C                     MOVE *OFF      STRERR
C                     ELSE
C                     Z-ADD0         STR1PS
C                     MOVE *ON       STRERR
C                     ENDIF
     *
C                     ENDSR
```

Determining the Size of a Field

Chapter 20

Use the techniques in this chapter to dynamically determine the length of any field and the number of decimal places in a numeric field.

For some coding techniques, you may need to know the declared size of a field. For example, to use the OS/400 APIs to edit a numeric field, you need to know the length and number of decimal places in the field. Or for dynamically building a string to display in a subfile (to provide a horizontal "panning" feature, for example), you'll need to know the length of each field being used. You could just hard-code these values; but when field sizes change, you have a maintenance nightmare. A much better approach is to dynamically determine field attributes at runtime using the following modules:

FLDLEN   provides a template for determining the size of any field (Figure 20.1).

FLDDP   provides a routine for determining the number of decimal places in a numeric field (Figure 20.2).

You will also need the STRDS, STRLEN, and STDCONST members from Chapter 16.

To determine the length of a field, add /COPY statements for STRDS and STDCONST at the end of the I-specs, and /COPY statements for STRLEN at the end of the C-specs. Then copy the FLDLEN template into your program and replace &fld with the name of the field and &len with a 3-digit numeric field to hold the length of &fld. To store the length of ORDAMT in AMTLEN, you would use the code

```
C                     MOVE *ZEROS    ORDAMT
C                     MOVELORDAMT    STR1        P
C                     EXSR STRLEN
C                     Z-ADDSTR1LN    AMTLEN
```

Determining the number of decimal places in a numeric field is just as easy. Add /COPY statements for STDCONST at the end of the I-specs, and /COPY statements for FLDDP at the end of the C-specs. To find the number of decimal places in ORDAMT and store the answer in AMTDP, you code

```
C                          Z-ADDDPMSK      ORDAMT
C                          Z-ADDORDAMT     DPTST
C                          EXSR FLDDP
C                          Z-ADDDP         AMTDP      30
```

Notice that both the techniques shown above overwrite the contents of a field. You can generally avoid problems caused by overwriting field contents by determining field sizes in your *INZSR initialization routine. If you use these routines in your code's mainline or in other subroutines, be sure to save field contents so that the contents can be restored after you use these routines.

Figure 20.1 FLDLEN Length of Field Template

```
... 1 ...+... 2 ...+... 3 ...+... 4 ...+... 5 ...+... 6 ...+... 7 ...+... 8

 *----------------------------------------------------------
 * FLDLEN    Length of field template
 *
 * Function:
 *   Return the declared length of a field. This function
 *   replaces the value of the field. Save and restore the
 *   field to preserve its value.
 *
 * Usage:
 *   Copy this template into your program and replace all
 *   &values listed below with your actual program variables.
 *
 * Requires copy modules:
 *   STRDS       Data structure for string functions
 *   STDCONST    Standard named constants
 *   STRLEN      Length of string function
 *
 * Expects:
 *   &fld        field
 *   &len        field_len
 *----------------------------------------------------------
C                          MOVE  *ZEROS     &fld
C                          MOVEL&fld        STR1       P
C                          EXSR  STRLEN
C                          Z-ADDSTR1LN      &len
```

Figure 20.2 FLDDP Decimal Positions in Numeric Field Function

```
... 1 ...+... 2 ...+... 3 ...+... 4 ...+... 5 ...+... 6 ...+... 7 ...+... 8

 *----------------------------------------------------------
 * FLDDP     Decimal positions in numeric field function
 *
 * Function:
 *   Return the decimal positions in a numeric field. This
 *   function replaces the value of the field. Save and restore
 *   the field to preserve its value.
 *
 * Requires copy module:
```

Figure 20.2 FLDDP Decimal Positions in Numeric Field Function, continued

```
... 1 ...+... 2 ...+... 3 ...+... 4 ...+... 5 ...+... 6 ...+... 7 ...+... 8

   *    STDCONST - Standard named constants
   *
   * Expects:
   *    DPTST  - dec_pos_test containing the value of field after
   *           - DPMSK (dec_pos_mask) assigned to field
   *
   * Returns:
   *    DP     - dec_pos
   *
   * Example:
   *    Calculate the number of decimal places in an amount field
   *    AMT and store the answer in AMTDP. Uses SVAMT to save the
   *    value of AMT.
   *
C*          *LIKE     DEFN AMT      SVAMT
C*                    Z-ADDAMT      SVAMT
   *
C*                    Z-ADDDPMSK    AMT
C*                    Z-ADDAMT      DPTST
C*                    EXSR FLDDP
C*                    Z-ADDDP       AMTDP   30
   *
C*                    Z-ADDSVAMT    AMT
   *
   *----------------------------------------------------------
C           FLDDP     BEGSR
   *
C                     Z-ADDDPTST    DPTST   99
C                     MOVELDPTST    @DPTST 10 P
   *
C           DPDGT     CHECK@DPTST   DP
C                     SUB  1        DP      30
   *
C                     ENDSR
```

Editing Numeric Fields

Chapter 21

With these two simple routines, you can edit any numeric value within an RPG program for output to a character field.

For most types of output, you can use edit codes on RPG O-specs or in a display file's DDS to edit numeric values. But suppose you want to embed an edited number in a string of text, or transfer numeric values to a remote system that doesn't support OS/400 data types. If you're ever faced with this kind of problem, try using the following /COPY modules:

EDTDS	provides the EDTDS data structure for editing a number (Figure 21.1).
EDTINZ	initializes an edit mask for a numeric field (Figure 21.2).
EDTNBR	edits a numeric field using the edit mask created by EDTINZ (Figure 21.3).

You will also need the ERRDS module shown in Figure 2.2 of Chapter 2. To use the modules, you code /COPY statements for the ERRDS and EDTDS data structures at the end of the I-specs, and /COPY statements for EDTINZ and EDTNBR at the end of the C-specs.

The routines provided in this chapter harness two OS/400 APIs, QECCVTEC and QECEDT. To edit a numeric value, first you use the EDTINZ routine (which calls the QECCVTEC API) to translate any valid RPG edit code into an edit mask for a particular numeric field. An edit mask is an overlay that is used to edit a field. It's best to execute EDTINZ from the *INZSR subroutine in your program so that it only runs once for each field you want to edit. Please note that EDTINZ needs to know the length and number of decimal places in the field you want to edit: Instead of hard-coding these values, look at the FLDLEN and FLDDP routines in Chapter 20 to see how to determine them dynamically at runtime.

To initialize the edit mask for the order amount in ORDAMT, of length AMTLEN with decimal places AMTDP, which is to be edited using the 'L' edit code, you code

```
C               *LIKE     DEFN EDTMSK    AMTMSK
C               *LIKE     DEFN EDTARG    AMTARG
  *
C                         MOVE 'L'       EDTCDE
C                         Z-ADDAMTLEN    EDTVLN
C                         Z-ADDAMTDP     EDTVDP
C                         EXSR EDTINZ
C                         MOVE EDTMSK    AMTMSK
C                         MOVE EDTARG    AMTARG
```

The EDTINZ routine returns two values: an edit mask that is saved in AMTMSK, and a set of editing arguments that is saved in AMTARG.

Once the edit mask has been created, you can use it as many times as you want to edit the ORDAMT field by adding the following code to execute the EDTNBR routine (which calls the QECEDT API):

```
C                         MOVELORDAMT    EDTVAR      P
C                         MOVE AMTMSK    EDTMSK
C                         MOVE AMTARG    EDTARG
C                         EXSR EDTNBR
C                         MOVELEDTSTR    AMTSTR 32 P
```

The edited value returned by the routine is stored in AMTSTR. The snippet of code above sizes AMTSTR larger than needed so that it contains enough room for the largest value ORDAMT can hold, with additional space for any edit characters inserted by the edit mask, such as a sign, commas, or a decimal point.

When you are using the EDTNBR function, it's important to remember that this function works just like the editing in your RPG O-specs or DDS. If the edit code you use specifies zero supression, then leading zeros in the output field will be replaced by blanks. If you want to concatenate the output into a text string, you will want to remove the leading blanks. For an easy way to do this, see the STRTRM function in Chapter 16, which trims leading blanks from a string.

Figure 21.1 EDTDS Data Structure for Edit Functions

```
... 1 ...+... 2 ...+... 3 ...+... 4 ...+... 5 ...+... 6 ...+... 7 ...+... 8

 *---------------------------------------------------------
 * EDTDS    Data structure for Edit functions
 *
 * Function:
 *   Defines parameters and constants for Edit functions.
 *
 * EDTDS      edit_API_DS:
 *   EDTMSK   edit_mask
 *   EDTARG   edit_args:
 *     EDTMLN   edit_mask_len
 *     EDTSLN   edit_str_len
 *     EDTFIL   edit_fill_char
 *     EDTCDE   edit_code
```

Figure 21.1 EDTDS Data Structure for Edit Functions, continued

```
... 1 ...+... 2 ...+... 3 ...+... 4 ...+... 5 ...+... 6 ...+... 7 ...+... 8

     *      EDTFLT    edit_float_char
     *      EDTVLN    edit_var_len
     *      EDTVDP    edit_var_dec_pos
     *   EDTVAR   edit_var
     *   EDTCLS   edit_var_class
     *   EDTSTR   edit_str
     *------------------------------------------------------------
IEDTDS       IDS
I                                          1 256 EDTMSK
 *
I                                        257 275 EDTARG
I                                      B 257 2600EDTMLN
I                                      B 261 2640EDTSLN
I                                        265 265 EDTFIL
I                                        266 266 EDTCDE
I                                        267 267 EDTFLT
I                                      B 268 2710EDTVLN
I                                      B 272 2750EDTVDP
 *
I                                        276 2900EDTVAR
I I            '*ZONED'                  291 300 EDTCLS
I                                        301 364 EDTSTR
```

Figure 21.2 EDTINZ Initialize Numeric Edit Function

```
... 1 ...+... 2 ...+... 3 ...+... 4 ...+... 5 ...+... 6 ...+... 7 ...+... 8

     *------------------------------------------------------------
     * EDTINZ    Initialize numeric edit function
     *
     * Function:
     *    Initializes the edit mask and arguments required by the
     *    Edit Number function EDTNBR. The edit mask may be created
     *    for any valid RPG edit code. Use the Field Length and
     *    Decimal Positions functions FLDLEN and FLDDP to obtain
     *    the declared size of the numeric field.
     *
     * Requires copy modules:
     *    EDTDS  - Data structure for Edit functions
     *    ERRDS  - Error data structure returned by APIs
     *
     * Expects:
     *    EDTCDE - edit_code
     *    EDTVLN - edit_var_len
     *    EDTVDP - edit_var_dec_pos
     *    EDTFLT - edit_float_char
     *
     * Returns:
     *    EDTMSK - edit_mask
     *    EDTARG - edit_args:
     *      EDTMLN - edit_mask_len
     *      EDTSLN - edit_str_len
```

Figure 21.2 EDTINZ Initialize Numeric Edit Function, continued

```
... 1 ...+... 2 ...+... 3 ...+... 4 ...+... 5 ...+... 6 ...+... 7 ...+... 8

     *     EDTFIL - edit_fill_char
     *     ERRDS  - err_API_DS
     *
     * Example:
     *     Initialize the edit mask AMTMSK and the edit arguments
     *     AMTARG for an amount field AMT, which is to be edited
     *     using the "L" edit code. The length and decimal positions
     *     in AMT have been calculated using the FLDLEN and FLDDP
     *     functions and stored in AMTLN and AMTDP.
     *
     C*          *LIKE    DEFN EDTMSK    AMTMSK
     C*          *LIKE    DEFN EDTARG    AMTARG
     *
     C*                   MOVE 'L'       EDTCDE
     C*                   Z-ADDAMTLN     EDTVLN
     C*                   Z-ADDAMTDP     EDTVDP
     C*                   EXSR EDTINZ
     C*                   MOVE EDTMSK    AMTMSK
     C*                   MOVE EDTARG    AMTARG
     *
     *-------------------------------------------------------------
     C           EDTINZ   BEGSR
     *
     C                    CALL 'QECCVTEC'
     C                    PARM           EDTMSK
     C                    PARM           EDTMLN
     C                    PARM           EDTSLN
     C                    PARM           EDTFIL
     C                    PARM           EDTCDE
     C                    PARM           EDTFLT
     C                    PARM           EDTVLN
     C                    PARM           EDTVDP
     C                    PARM           ERRDS
     *
     * Clear optional arguments
     *
     C                    MOVE *BLANKS   EDTFLT
     *
     C                    ENDSR
```

Figure 21.3 EDTNBR Edit Number Function

```
... 1 ...+... 2 ...+... 3 ...+... 4 ...+... 5 ...+... 6 ...+... 7 ...+... 8

     *-------------------------------------------------------------
     * EDTNBR - Edit number function
     *
     * Function:
     *    Edits a number using the edit mask and arguments created
     *    by the Initialize Edit function EDTINZ.
     *
     * Requires copy modules:
```

Figure 21.3 EDTNBR Edit Number Function, continued

```
... 1 ...+... 2 ...+... 3 ...+... 4 ...+... 5 ...+... 6 ...+... 7 ...+... 8
 *     EDTDS  - Data structure for Edit functions
 *     ERRDS  - Error data structure returned by APIs
 *     INZEDT - Initialize numeric edit function
 *
 * Expects:
 *     EDTVAR - edit_var
 *     EDTMSK - edit_mask
 *     EDTARG - edit_args
 *
 * Returns:
 *     EDTSTR - edit_str
 *     ERRDS  - err_API_DS
 *
 * Example:
 *     Edit an amount field AMT, using the edit mask AMTMSK and
 *     edit arguments AMTARG created by EDTINZ, and store the
 *     edited value in the string AMTSTR.
 *
C*                      MOVELAMT        EDTVAR
C*                      MOVE AMTMSK     EDTMSK
C*                      MOVE AMTARG     EDTARG
C*                      EXSR EDTNBR
C*                      MOVELEDTSTR     AMTSTR 32 P
 *
 *-----------------------------------------------------------------
C          EDTNBR      BEGSR
 *
C                      MOVE *BLANKS    EDTSTR
 *
C                      CALL 'QECEDT'
C                      PARM            EDTSTR
C                      PARM            EDTSLN
C                      PARM            EDTVAR
C                      PARM            EDTCLS
C                      PARM            EDTVLN
C                      PARM            EDTMSK
C                      PARM            EDTMLN
C                      PARM            EDTFIL
C                      PARM            ERRDS
 *
C                      ENDSR
```

Reformatting Numeric Data

Chapter 22

Use this routine to translate a numeric value in a string into a numeric field.

Client/server applications are often complicated by the incompatability between the data types allowed on the client and server platforms. You may find your AS/400 receives numeric data from a client, such as a PC or an RS/6000, in an edited format that includes a sign and embedded decimal point, rather than in the signed-numeric format with assumed decimal point you are used to. For this situation, you need a routine for converting such edited data into numeric values you can process in your RPG programs. The NBRFMT routine presented in this chapter (Figure 22.1) does just that. NBRFMT accepts a string that contains an edited number and converts that edited number to a numeric field. To use NBRFMT, you will also need the STDCONST /COPY module from Chapter 16.

We've designed NBRFMT to be as simple as possible. The routine can accept a string of up to 32 characters, which can contain

- leading and trailing blanks
- an optional leading or trailing sign
- an integer value
- a decimal point
- a decimal value

The routine can reformat this string as a number up to 15 digits long. The routine checks for invalid numeric data and integer truncation, and returns an error if either occurs. Just like the edit routines in the previous chapter, NBRFMT needs to know the length and number of decimal places in the number to be formatted. Although you could hard-code these values, we strongly recommend you use the FLDLEN and FLDDP routines in Chapter 20 to dynamically determine them at runtime.

To use NBRFMT, you add a /COPY statement for STDCONST at the end of your I-specs, and a /COPY statement for NBRFMT at the end of the C-specs. To reformat the value in AMTSTR into signed-numeric field ORDAMT, of length AMTLEN with decimal places AMTDP, you code

```
C                           MOVELAMTSTR    NBRSTR    P
C                           Z-ADDAMTLEN    NBRLEN
C                           Z-ADDAMTDP     NBRDP
C                           MOVE *ON       NBRSGN
C                           EXSR NBRFMT
  *
C              NBRERR       IFEQ *OFF
C                           MOVE NBR       ORDAMT
C                           ELSE
  :                         handle error
C                           ENDIF
```

NBRFMT returns the number into NBR, which is then moved to ORDAMT. The decimal places in NBRDP and the sign in NBRSGN are optional; both can be omitted when not required, to simplify the reformatting of unsigned integer fields.

Figure 22.1 NBRFMT Format Number from String Function

```
... 1 ...+... 2 ...+... 3 ...+... 4 ...+... 5 ...+... 6 ...+... 7 ...+... 8

*-----------------------------------------------------------
* NBRFMT    Format number from string function
*
*
* Function:
*   Formats a number from a string that may include leading
*   and trailing blanks, a leading or trailing sign, an
*   integer value, a decimal point, and decimal places. Use
*   the Field Length and Decimal Positions functions FLDLEN
*   and FLDDP to obtain the declared size of the field.
*
* Requires copy modules:
*   STDCONST - Standard named constants
*
* Expects:
*   NBRSTR - number_str
*   NBRLEN - number_len
*   NBRDP  - number_dec_pos (optional)
*   NBRSGN - number_signed (optional)
*
* Returns:
*   NBR    - number
*   NBRERR - number_error
*
* Example:
*   Format an amount field AMT from a string AMTSTR. The
*   length and decimal positions in AMT have been calculated
*   using the FLDLEN and FLDDP functions and stored in AMTLN
*   and AMTDP. AMT may be signed.
*
```

Figure 22.1 NBRFMT Format Number from String Function, continued

```
... 1 ...+... 2 ...+... 3 ...+... 4 ...+... 5 ...+... 6 ...+... 7 ...+... 8
C*                      MOVELAMTSTR    NBRSTR    P
C*                      Z-ADDAMTLN     NBRLEN
C*                      Z-ADDAMTDP     NBRDP
C*                      MOVE *ON       NBRSGN
C*                      EXSR NBRFMT
  *
C*         NBRERR       IFEQ *OFF
C*                      MOVE NBR       AMT
C*                      ELSE
  *                     ...
C*                      ENDIF
  *

  *-------------------------------------------------------
C          NBRFMT       BEGSR
  *
  * Declare variables
  *
C                       Z-ADD0         NBR      150
C                       MOVE NBRLEN    NBRLEN    30
C                       MOVE NBRDP     NBRDP     30
C                       MOVE NBRSGN    NBRSGN    1
C                       MOVE NBRSTR    NBRSTR   32
C                       MOVE *OFF      NBRERR    1
  *
C                       MOVELNBRSTR    @NSTR     33
C                       MOVE EOSTR     @NSTR
C                       Z-ADD33        @NEOS     30
C                       MOVE *ZEROS    @NNBR     15
C                       Z-ADD15        @NSIZ     30
C                       Z-ADD1         @NP       30
C                       Z-ADD1         @NN       30
C                       Z-ADD0         @NI       30
C                       MOVE *BLANKS   @NINT     32
C                       Z-ADD0         @ND       30
C                       MOVE *ZEROS    @NDEC     32
C                       MOVE *BLANKS   @NSGN     1
  *
  * A number may include leading and trailing blanks, leading or
  * trailing sign, integers, decimal point, and decimals.
  *
  * Bypass leading blanks
  *
C                       Z-ADD@NN       @NP
C          BLK          CHECK@NSTR:@NP @NN
  *
  * Check for leading sign
  *
C                       Z-ADD@NN       @NP
C          SGNC         CHECK@NSTR:@NP @NN
C          @NN          IFGT @NP
C          1            SUBST@NSTR:@NP @NSGN
C          @NP          ADD  1         @NN
```

```
C                     ENDIF
 *
 * Check for integers
 *
C                     Z-ADD@NN      @NP
C         DGTC        CHECK@NSTR:@NP @NN
C         @NN         IFGT @NP
C         @NN         SUB  @NP      @NI
C         @NI         SUBST@NSTR:@NP @NINT
C                     ENDIF
 *
 * Check for decimal point
 *
C                     Z-ADD@NN      @NP
C         DPC         CHECK@NSTR:@NP @NN
C         @NN         IFGT @NP
C         @NP         ADD  1        @NN
C                     ENDIF
 *
 * Check for decimals
 *
C                     Z-ADD@NN      @NP
C         DGTC        CHECK@NSTR:@NP @NN
C         @NN         IFGT @NP
C         @NN         SUB  @NP      @ND
C         @ND         SUBST@NSTR:@NP @NDEC
C                     ENDIF
 *
 * Check for trailing sign
 *
C         @NSGN       IFEQ *BLANKS
C                     Z-ADD@NN      @NP
C         SGNC        CHECK@NSTR:@NP @NN
C         @NN         IFGT @NP
C         1           SUBST@NSTR:@NP @NSGN
C         @NP         ADD  1        @NN
C                     ENDIF
C                     ENDIF
 *
 * Bypass trailing blanks
 *
C                     Z-ADD@NN      @NP
C         BLK         CHECK@NSTR:@NP @NN
 *
 * Error if next pointer not at end of string
 *
C         @NN         IFNE @NEOS
C                     MOVE *ON      NBRERR
C                     ENDIF
 *
 * Error if length out of range or integer truncation, or
 * not signed and negative, but allow decimal truncation
```

Figure 22.1 NBRFMT Format Number from String Function, continued

```
... 1 ...+... 2 ...+... 3 ...+... 4 ...+... 5 ...+... 6 ...+... 7 ...+... 8
     *
C           NBRLEN    SUB  NBRDP    @NP
C           NBRLEN    IFLT 1
C           NBRLEN    ORGT @NSIZ
C           NBRLEN    ORLT NBRDP
C           @NI       ORGT @NP
C           NBRSGN    ORNE *ON
C           @NSGN     ANDEQMINUS
C                     MOVE *ON      NBRERR
C                     ENDIF
     *
     * Format number when no errors found
     *
C           NBRERR    IFEQ *OFF
     *
C           @NSIZ     SUB  NBRDP    @NP
C                     SUB  @NI      @NP
       C             @NP       IFNE 0
C           @NP       SUBST@NNBR:1  @NNBR      P
C                     ELSE
C                     CLEAR@NNBR
C                     ENDIF
C                     CAT  @NINT:0  @NNBR
C                     CAT  @NDEC:0  @NNBR
C                     MOVE @NNBR    NBR
C           @NSGN     IFEQ MINUS
C                     Z-SUBNBR      NBR
C                     ENDIF
     *
C                     ENDIF
     *
     * Clear optional arguments
     *
C                     Z-ADD0        NBRDP
C                     MOVE *OFF     NBRSGN
     *
C                     ENDSR
```

Reformatting Dates

Chapter 23

Use these modules to reformat and validate dates.

After character and numeric variables, dates are the most commonly used data type in business applications. You will find home-grown routines in most programs for reformatting or validating dates. In this chapter, we show you a simple function for converting dates from one format to another. You can also use this function to validity-check date fields. The modules we present in this chapter are

DATDS	provides the DATDS data structure and named constants required by DATCNT and DATCVT (Figure 23.1).
DATCNT	returns the century indicator for a date (Figure 23.2).
DATCVT	uses the OS/400 QWCCVTDT API to convert a date from one format to another (Figure 23.3).

You will also need module ERRDS from Figure 2.2 of Chapter 2.

To use the modules, you include the ERRDS and DATDS data structures at the end of the I-specs. The DATDS module (Figure 23.1) defines the input and output variables for the DATCVT function and the date formats that DATCVT supports. All date formats require a century indicator as well as a date: Use named constant DTC20 (or '0') for the twentieth century; use named constant DTC21 (or '1') for the twenty-first century. For dates without an associated century indicator, you can use the DATCNT function (Figure 23.2) to return a century indicator. DATCNT expects dates in year-month-day format and returns DTC20 for years 40 to 99, or DTC21 for years 00 to 39. To return a century indicator for an order date, ORDDAT, add a copy statement for the DATCNT module at the end of the C-specs, and then code

```
C           *LIKE     DEFN DTCNTO    ORDCNT
  *
C                     MOVE ORDDAT    DTDATI
C                     EXSR DATCNT
C                     MOVE DTCNTO    ORDCNT
```

Once a date field has an associated century indicator, you can use the DATCVT function (Figure 23.3) to convert it into any format. To convert ORDDAT from year-month-day (DTFYMD) to your system format (DTFSYS), add a /COPY statement for the DATCVT module at the end of the C-specs, and then code

```
C                     MOVE ORDCNT    DTCNTI
C                     MOVE ORDDAT    DTDATI
C                     MOVE DTFYMD    DTFMTI
C                     MOVE DTFSYS    DTFMTO
C                     EXSR DATCVT
  *
C           DTERR     IFEQ *OFF
C                     MOVE DTCNTO    ORDCNT
C                     MOVE DTDATO    ORDDAT
C                     ELSE
  :                   handle error here
C                     ENDIF
```

The DATCVT function returns an error field, DTERR, if the input date is invalid. As a result, you can use DATCVT to validate date fields as well as to convert them. For example, if your order-entry program accepts an order date from a display file in system format (DTFSYS), you code the following to validate and convert it to DTFYMD format:

```
C                     MOVE DTC20     DTCNTI
C                     MOVE ORDDAT    DTDATI
C                     MOVE DTFSYS    DTFMTI
C                     MOVE DTFYMD    DTFMTO
C                     EXSR DATCVT
  *
C           DTERR     IFEQ *OFF
C                     MOVE DTDATO    ORDDAT
C                     MOVE ORDDAT    DTDATI
C                     EXSR DATCNT
C                     MOVE DTCNTO    ORDCNT
C                     ELSE
  :                   handle error here
C                     ENDIF
```

Notice how we use DTC20 as dummy input for DATCVT, and then use DATCNT to return the actual century indicator for ORDDAT once it is in year-month-day format. This technique allows the user to enter a 6-character date, from which the program calculates the corresponding century indicator.

We should point out one limitation to the DATCVT function. The QWCCVTDT API used by the subroutine only supports century indicators for the twentieth and twenty-first centuries. We haven't found any problems with this approach; but if your system stores dates outside this range, say for a catalog of old master paintings, you will have to use another technique for reformatting dates that supports a full 4-digit year.

Figure 23.1 DATDS Data Structure for Date Functions

```
... 1 ...+... 2 ...+... 3 ...+... 4 ...+... 5 ...+... 6 ...+... 7 ...+... 8

*---------------------------------------------------------------
* DATDS   Data structure for Date functions
*
* Function:
*    Defines parameters and constants for Date functions.
*
* DATDS       date_DS:
*    DTFMTI   date_in_format
*    DTVARI   date_in_var:
*      DTCNTI   date_in_cent
*      DTDATI   date_in_date
*       DTJULI   date_in_julian
*      DTTIMI   date_in_time
*      DTMLSI   date_in_millisecs
*    DTFMTO   date_out_format
*    DTVARO   date_out_var:
*      DTCNTO   date_out_cent
*      DTDATO   date_out_date
*       DTJULO   date_out_julian
*      DTTIMO   date_out_time
*      DTMLSO   date_out_millisecs
*---------------------------------------------------------------
IDATDS       IDS
I                                         1  10 DTFMTI
I                                        11  26 DTVARI
I                                        11  11 DTCNTI
I                                        12  17 DTDATI
I                                        12  16 DTJULI
I                                        18  23 DTTIMI
I                                        24  26 DTMLSI
 *
I                                        27  36 DTFMTO
I                                        37  52 DTVARO
I                                        37  37 DTCNTO
I                                        38  43 DTDATO
I                                        38  42 DTJULO
I                                        44  49 DTTIMO
I                                        50  52 DTMLSO
 *
*---------------------------------------------------------------
*    DTFCUR   date_fmt_curr_clock   cent, date, time, millisecs
*    DTFDTS   date_fmt_time_stamp   cent, date, time, millisecs
*    DTFJOB   date_fmt_job          cent, date
*    DTFSYS   date_fmt_sys_val      cent, date
*    DTFYMD   date_fmt_YMD          cent, date
```

Figure 23.1 DATDS Data Structure for Date Functions, continued

```
... 1 ...+... 2 ...+... 3 ...+... 4 ...+... 5 ...+... 6 ...+... 7 ...+... 8

 *    DTFMDY     date_fmt_MDY            cent, date
 *    DTFDMY     date_fmt_DMY            cent, date
 *    DTFJUL     date_fmt_julian         cent, julian
 *    DTC20      date_cent_20
 *    DTC21      date_cent_21
 *------------------------------------------------------------
I                '*CURRENT '              C         DTFCUR
I                '*DTS     '              C         DTFDTS
I                '*JOB     '              C         DTFJOB
I                '*SYSVAL  '              C         DTFSYS
I                '*YMD     '              C         DTFYMD
I                '*MDY     '              C         DTFMDY
I                '*DMY     '              C         DTFDMY
I                '*JUL     '              C         DTFJUL
I                '0'                      C         DTC20
I                '1'                      C         DTC21
```

Figure 23.2 DATCNT Return Century Indicator for Date Function

```
... 1 ...+... 2 ...+... 3 ...+... 4 ...+... 5 ...+... 6 ...+... 7 ...+... 8

 *----------------------------------------------------------
 * DATCNT    Return century indicator for date function
 *
 * Function:
 *    Return the century indicator for a date. The date must be
 *    in YMD format. Returns DTC20 for the 20th century if the
 *    year is greater than 39, else DTC21 for the 21st century.
 *
 * Requires copy modules:
 *    DATDS     Data structure for Date functions
 *
 * Expects:
 *    DTDATI    date_in_date (in YMD format)
 *
 * Returns:
 *    DTCNTO    date_out_cent
 *    DTERR     date_err on error
 *
 * Example:
 *    Return the century indicator for the current date in CURDAT
 *    and store the result in CURCNT.
 *
C*          *LIKE     DEFN DTCNTO      CURCNT
 *
C*                    MOVE CURDAT      DTDATI
C*                    EXSR DATCNT
C*                    MOVE DTCNTO      CURCNT
 *
 *----------------------------------------------------------
C           DATCNT    BEGSR
 *
```

Figure 23.2 DATCNT Return Century Indicator for Date Function, continued

```
... 1 ...+... 2 ...+... 3 ...+... 4 ...+... 5 ...+... 6 ...+... 7 ...+... 8

C                       MOVE *OFF      DTERR   1
C                       MOVE @DTPOS    @DTPOS  30
 *
C           DGTC        CHECKDTDATI    @DTPOS
 *
C                       SELEC
 *
C           @DTPOS      WHNE 0
C                       MOVE *ON       DTERR
 *
C           DTDATI      WHGE '400000'
C                       MOVE DTC20     DTCNTO
 *
C                       OTHER
C                       MOVE DTC21     DTCNTO
 *
C                       ENDSL
 *
C                       ENDSR
```

Figure 23.3 DATCVT Convert Date Function

```
... 1 ...+... 2 ...+... 3 ...+... 4 ...+... 5 ...+... 6 ...+... 7 ...+... 8

 *----------------------------------------------------------
 * DATCVT    Convert date function
 *
 * Function:
 *   Convert a date from one format to another. See the named
 *   constants at the end of copy member DATDS for the possible
 *   formats. The date must have an associated century code.
 *   Use the Retrieve Century function DATCNT for dates that
 *   do not have a century code.
 *
 * Requires copy modules:
 *   DATDS  - Data structure for Date functions
 *   ERRDS  - Error data structure returned by APIs
 *
 * Expects:
 *   DTFMTI - date_in_format
 *   DTVARI - date_in_var:
 *     DTCNTI - date_in_cent
 *     DTDATI - date_in_date
 *       DTJULI - date_in_julian
 *     DTTIMI - date_in_time
 *     DTMLSI - date_in_millisecs
 *   DTFMTO - date_out_format
 *
 * Returns:
 *   DTVARO - date_out_var:
 *     DTCNTO - date_out_cent
 *     DTDATO - date_out_date
```

Figure 23.3 DATCVT Convert Date Function, continued

```
 ... 1 ...+... 2 ...+... 3 ...+... 4 ...+... 5 ...+... 6 ...+... 7 ...+... 8

     *     DTJULO - date_out_julian
     *     DTTIMO - date_out_time
     *     DTMLSO - date_out_millisecs
     *   DTERR  - date_err on error
     *   ERRDS  - err_API_DS describing error
     *
     * Example:
     *   Convert the current date in CURDAT, of century CURCNT,
     *   from YMD format to Julian format, and store the result
     *   in CURJUL.
     *
C*                       MOVE CURCNT     DTCNTI
C*                       MOVE CURDAT     DTDATI
C*                       MOVE DTFYMD     DTFMTI
C*                       MOVE DTFJUL     DTFMTO
C*                       EXSR DATCVT
     *
C*          DTERR        IFEQ *OFF
C*                       MOVE DTCNTO     CURCNT
C*                       MOVE DTJULO     CURJUL
C*                       ELSE
     *                   ...
C*                       ENDIF
     *
     *------------------------------------------------------------
C           DATCVT       BEGSR
     *
C                        MOVE *OFF       DTERR    1
     *
C                        CALL 'QWCCVTDT'
C                        PARM            DTFMTI
C                        PARM            DTVARI
C                        PARM            DTFMTO
C                        PARM            DTVARO
C                        PARM            ERRDS
     *
C           ERRDLN       IFGT 0
C                        MOVE *ON        DTERR
C                        ENDIF
     *
C                        ENDSR
```

Doing Date Arithmetic

Chapter 24

Learn the basics of date arithmetic with two simple programs: ZDATADD adds or subtracts a number of days from a date; ZDATDIF calculates the difference in days between two dates.

Date arithmetic is an absolute must for many applications. An inventory application needs to add the lead time for a product to the purchase order date to find the expected receipt date. For sales order processing, you may want to analyze performance by looking at the difference between the actual and planned shipment dates for each order. In this chapter, we show you two programs for solving these problems; but first we'll explain the design of our date arithmetic routines. This background knowledge will not only help you understand the code but will also give you the basics for writing your own date routines.

The main problem with dates is finding some universal format in which they can be manipulated. Because the date routines in the previous chapter support dates in the twentieth and twenty-first century, we decided to convert dates into days, taking January 1, 1900, as our base point, or day 1. We knew that once dates were in this universal format, date arithmetic would be easy. To add days to a date, convert the date to universal format, add the days, then convert back to Gregorian format. To find the difference between two dates, convert the dates to universal format, then subtract one from the other.

To simplify the conversion from Gregorian to universal format, we decided to split the process into two steps. We first use the DATCVT routine from the previous chapter to convert from year-month-day to a Julian date, which consists of a 2-digit year, followed by a 3-digit day in the year. Then we use the DATJ2U routine (Figure 24.1) to convert from Julian to universal format. To convert from universal back to Gregorian, we just reverse the process. First convert from universal to Julian using the DATU2J routine (Figure 24.2). Then use DATCVT to convert from Julian back to year-month-day.

It took us a while to get the code for DATJ2U and DATU2J right. A quick glance at the routines (Figures 24.1 and 24.2) shows that they rely on multiplication and division by 365.25 to round the result correctly. Obviously, this type of coding needs thorough testing — random testing is not sufficient. So we wrote a program to test the algorithms with every date from January 1, 1900, to December 31, 2099. Remember when you write similar programs to test them thoroughly. It's far easier to test programs during development than to try to debug them once they are in production.

Let's now look at the date arithmetic programs to see how the routines are used. Program ZDATADD (Figure 24.3) adds days to a date. To subtract days from a date, you make the number of days negative. ZDATADD simply consists of a comment header section and a short mainline that uses /COPY routines we've already developed, such as DATJ2U and DAT2UJ. As you can see, the simplicity of the program allows you to focus on its primary function without getting bogged down in the details of the secondary /COPY routines.

Using ZDATADD is simple. To add the lead time for a product in LDTIM to a purchase order date in PORDAT, to find the scheduled receipt date in PRCDAT, you code

```
C                         MOVE PORCNT    INCNT
C                         MOVE PORDAT    INDAT
C                         Z-ADDLDTIM     INDAY
     *
C                         CALL  'ZDATADD'
C                         PARM           INCNT  10
C                         PARM           INDAT  60
C                         PARM           INDAY  50
C                         PARM           OUTCNT 10
C                         PARM           OUTDAT 60
C                         PARM           ERRDS
     *
C           ERRDLN        IFEQ 0
C                         MOVE OUTCNT    PRCCNT
C                         MOVE OUTDAT    PRCDAT
C                         ELSE
     :                    handle error here
C                         ENDIF
```

Just like the date routines in the last chapter, ZDATADD requires a century indicator for each date that is passed to it: PORCNT for PORDAT; PRCCNT for PRCDAT.

To find the difference between two dates, you call the ZDATDIF program (Figure 24.4). For example, to calculate the number of days between the scheduled shipment date for an order in OSCDAT and the actual shipment date in OACDAT, and then store the result in DIFDAY, you code

```
C                          MOVE OSCCNT     INCNT1
C                          MOVE OSCDAT     INDAT1
C                          MOVE OACCNT     INCNT2
C                          MOVE OACDAT     INDAT2
 *
C                          CALL 'ZDATDIF'
C                          PARM            INCNT1 10
C                          PARM            INDAT1 60
C                          PARM            INCNT2 10
C                          PARM            INDAT2 60
C                          PARM            OUTDIF 50
C                          PARM            ERRDS
 *
C          ERRDLN  IFEQ 0
C                  Z-ADDOUTDIF     DIFDAY
C                  ELSE
     :             handle error here
C                  ENDIF
```

If the actual date is later than the scheduled date, the result is positive. If the actual date is earlier than the scheduled date, the result is negative. If both dates are the same, the result is zero.

You can easily write your own date functions using the /COPY modules in this chapter and Chapter 23. For example, you might need a function that calculates the day of the week for any date. To do this, first find out the day of the week for our base date of January 1, 1900. Then convert any date to universal format and divide by 7; a result of 0 means the date was on the base day; for any other result, just count forward from the base day.

Figure 24.1 DATJ2U Convert Date from Julian to Universal Format Function

```
... 1 ...+... 2 ...+... 3 ...+... 4 ...+... 5 ...+... 6 ...+... 7 ...+... 8

*----------------------------------------------------------
* DATJ2U    Convert date from Julian to Universal format function
*
* Function:
*    Convert a date from Julian format to Universal format. The
*    Universal format is the number of days since 1st Jan 1900.
*    Use the Convert Date function DATCVT to convert the input
*    date to Julian format if required.
*
* Requires copy modules:
*    DATDS      - Data structure for Date functions
*    STDCONST - Standard named constants
*
* Expects:
*    DTVARI - date_in_var:
*       DTCNTI - date_in_cent
*       DTJULI - date_in_julian
*
* Returns:
```

Figure 24.1 DATJ2U Convert Date from Julian to Universal Format Function, continued

```
... 1 ...+... 2 ...+... 3 ...+... 4 ...+... 5 ...+... 6 ...+... 7 ...+... 8

     *   DTDATO - date_out_date in Universal format
     *   DTERR  - date_err on error
     *
     * Example:
     *   Convert the current Julian date in CURJUL, of century
     *   CURCNT, into Universal format and store the result in
     *   CURUDT.
     *
C*                     MOVE CURCNT    DTCNTI
C*                     MOVE CURJUL    DTJULI
C*                     EXSR DATJ2U
C*                     MOVE DTDATO    CURUDT
     *
     *---------------------------------------------------------
C          DATJ2U      BEGSR
     *
C                      MOVE *OFF      DTERR   1
C                      MOVE @DTPOS    @DTPOS  30
C                      MOVE @DTUNV    @DTUNV  60
C                      MOVE @DTCYR    @DTCYR  30
C                      MOVE @DTDAY    @DTDAY  30
     *
C          DGTC        CHECKDTJULI    @DTPOS
     *
     * If no errors, split into century/year and day in year, then
     * convert to Universal format
     *
C                      SELEC
     *
C          @DTPOS      WHNE 0
C          DTCNTI      ORLT '0'
C          DTCNTI      ORGT '1'
C                      MOVE *ON       DTERR
     *
C                      OTHER
C                      MOVELDTVARI    @DTCYR
C                      MOVE DTJULI    @DTDAY
C          @DTCYR      SUB  1         @DTUNV
C                      MULT 365.25    @DTUNV
C                      ADD  365       @DTUNV
C                      ADD  @DTDAY    @DTUNV
C                      MOVE @DTUNV    DTDATO
     *
C                      ENDSL
     *
C                      ENDSR
```

Figure 24.2 DATU2J Convert Date from Universal to Julian Format Function

```
... 1 ...+... 2 ...+... 3 ...+... 4 ...+... 5 ...+... 6 ...+... 7 ...+... 8

 *----------------------------------------------------------
 * DATU2J   Convert date from Universal to Julian format function
 *
 * Function:
 *   Convert a date from Universal format to Julian format. The
 *   Universal format is the number of days since 1st Jan 1900.
 *   Use the Convert Date function DATCVT to convert the output
 *   date from Julian format if required.
 *
 * Requires copy modules:
 *   DATDS    - Data structure for Date functions
 *   STDCONST - Standard named constants
 *
 * Expects:
 *   DTDATI - date_in_date in Universal format
 *
 * Returns:
 *   DTVARO - date_out_var:
 *     DTCNTO - date_out_cent
 *     DTJULO - date_out_julian
 *   DTERR  - date_err on error
 *
 * Example:
 *   Convert the current Universal date in CURUDT into Julian
 *   format and store the result in CURCNT and CURJUL.
 *
C*                   MOVE CURUDT    DTDATI
C*                   EXSR DATU2J
C*                   MOVE DTCNTO    CURCNT
C*                   MOVE DTJULO    CURJUL
 *
 *----------------------------------------------------------
C          DATU2J    BEGSR
 *
C                    MOVE *OFF      DTERR    1
C                    MOVE @DTPOS    @DTPOS   30
C                    MOVE @DTUNV    @DTUNV   60
C                    MOVE @DTCYR    @DTCYR   30
C                    MOVE @DTDAY    @DTDAY   30
 *
C          DGTC      CHECKDTDATI    @DTPOS
 *
 * If no errors, convert to century/year and day in year, then
 * concatenate into Julian format
 *
C                    SELEC
 *
C          @DTPOS    WHNE 0
C                    MOVE *ON       DTERR
 *
C                    OTHER
C                    MOVE DTDATI    @DTUNV
```

Figure 24.2 DATU2J Convert Date from Universal to Julian Format Function, continued

```
... 1 ...+... 2 ...+... 3 ...+... 4 ...+... 5 ...+... 6 ...+... 7 ...+... 8

C           @DTUNV    DIV  365.25    @DTCYR
C                     MVR            @DTDAY
C           @DTCYR    IFGT 0
C                     ADD  1         @DTDAY
C                     ENDIF
C                     MOVE @DTDAY    DTJULO
C                     MOVEL@DTCYR    DTVARO
  *
C                     ENDSL
  *
C                     ENDSR
```

Figure 24.3 ZDATADD Add Days to Date

```
... 1 ...+... 2 ...+... 3 ...+... 4 ...+... 5 ...+... 6 ...+... 7 ...+... 8


 *-----------------------------------------------------------
 * ZDATADD    Add days to date
 *
 * Function:
 *   Adds a number of days to a date in YMD format. The number
 *   of days may be either positive or negative.
 *
 * Parameters:
 *   INCNT  - in_cent
 *   INDAT  - in_date
 *   INDAY  - in_days
 *   OUTCNT - out_cent
 *   OUTDAT - out_date
 *   ERRDS  - err_API_DS on error
 *
 * Example:
 *   Add 7 days to the current date in CURDAT, of century
 *   CURCNT.
 *
C*                    MOVE CURCNT    INCNT
C*                    MOVE CURDAT    INDAT
C*                    Z-ADD7         INDAY
 *
C*                    CALL 'ZDATADD'
C*                    PARM           INCNT    10
C*                    PARM           INDAT    60
C*                    PARM           INDAY    50
C*                    PARM           OUTCNT   10
C*                    PARM           OUTDAT   60
C*                    PARM           ERRDS
 *
C*          ERRDLN    IFEQ 0
C*                    MOVE OUTCNT    CURCNT
C*                    MOVE OUTDAT    CURDAT
C*                    ELSE
```

Figure 24.3 ZDATADD Add Days to Date, continued

```
... 1 ...+... 2 ...+... 3 ...+... 4 ...+... 5 ...+... 6 ...+... 7 ...+... 8
 *                       ...
C*                       ENDIF
 *
 *-----------------------------------------------------------
 *
 *-----------------------------------------------------------
 * Copy input modules
 *-----------------------------------------------------------
/COPY DATDS
/COPY ERRDS
/COPY PGMSDS
/COPY RERDS
/COPY STDCONST
 *
 *-----------------------------------------------------------
 * Entry point
 *-----------------------------------------------------------
C           *ENTRY    PLIST
C                     PARM            INCNT   10
C                     PARM            INDAT   60
C                     PARM            INDAY   50
C                     PARM            OUTCNT  10
C                     PARM            OUTDAT  60
C                     PARM            RERDS
 *
 *-----------------------------------------------------------
 * Mainline
 *-----------------------------------------------------------
 *
 * Check for required number of parameters
 *
C           PSPRMS    IFLT 5
C                     MOVE *ON        *INLR
C                     RETRN
C                     ENDIF
 *
 * Initialize variables
 *
C                     RESETERRDS
C                     Z-ADD6          ERRPRM
C                     Z-ADD0          OUTCNT
C                     Z-ADD0          OUTDAT
C                     Z-ADD0          WKUNV   60
 *
 * Convert from YMD to Julian to Universal
 *
C                     MOVE INCNT      DTCNTI
C                     MOVE INDAT      DTDATI
C                     MOVE DTFYMD     DTFMTI
C                     MOVE DTFJUL     DTFMTO
C                     EXSR DATCVT
 *
```

Figure 24.3 ZDATADD Add Days to Date, continued

```
... 1 ...+... 2 ...+... 3 ...+... 4 ...+... 5 ...+... 6 ...+... 7 ...+... 8

C           DTERR       IFEQ *OFF
C                       MOVE DTVARO     DTVARI
C                       EXSR DATJ2U
C                       MOVELDTDATO     WKUNV
C                       ENDIF
 *
 * Add days to date
 *
C           DTERR       IFEQ *OFF
C                       ADD  INDAY      WKUNV
C                       ENDIF
 *
 * Convert from Universal to Julian to YMD
 *
C           DTERR       IFEQ *OFF
C                       MOVELWKUNV      DTDATI
C                       EXSR DATU2J
C                       ENDIF
 *
C           DTERR       IFEQ *OFF
C                       MOVE DTVARO     DTVARI
C                       MOVE DTFJUL     DTFMTI
C                       MOVE DTFYMD     DTFMTO
C                       EXSR DATCVT
C                       MOVE DTCNTO     OUTCNT
C                       MOVE DTDATO     OUTDAT
C                       ENDIF
 *
 * Set return error
 *
C                       EXSR RERSET
 *
C                       RETRN
 *
 *-----------------------------------------------------------
 * Copy calc modules
 *-----------------------------------------------------------
 /COPY DATCVT
 /COPY DATJ2U
 /COPY DATU2J
 /COPY RERSET
```

Figure 24.4 ZDATDIF Difference Between Dates

```
... 1 ...+... 2 ...+... 3 ...+... 4 ...+... 5 ...+... 6 ...+... 7 ...+... 8

 *-----------------------------------------------------------
 * ZDATDIF    Difference between dates
 *
 * Function:
 *   Calculates the difference in days between two dates in YMD
 *   format. If the first date is earlier than the second date,
```

Figure 24.4 ZDATDIF Difference Between Dates, continued

```
... 1 ...+... 2 ...+... 3 ...+... 4 ...+... 5 ...+... 6 ...+... 7 ...+... 8

     *    the difference is positive. If the first date is later than
     *    the second date, the difference is negative.
     *
     * Parameters:
     *    INCNT1 - in_cent1
     *    INDAT1 - in_date1
     *    INCNT2 - in_cent2
     *    INDAT2 - in_date2
     *    OUTDIF - out_diff
     *    ERRDS  - err_API_DS on error
     *
     * Example:
     *    Calculate the difference between the current date in
     *    CURDAT, of century CURCNT, and the last month end date
     *    in CLODAT, of century CLOCNT, and store the result in
     *    DIFDAY.
     *
     C*                    MOVE CLOCNT    INCNT1
     C*                    MOVE CLODAT    INDAT1
     C*                    MOVE CURCNT    INCNT2
     C*                    MOVE CURDAT    INDAT2
     *
     C*                    CALL 'ZDATDIF'
     C*                    PARM           INCNT1 10
     C*                    PARM           INDAT1 60
     C*                    PARM           INCNT2 10
     C*                    PARM           INDAT2 60
     C*                    PARM           OUTDIF 50
     C*                    PARM           ERRDS
     *
     C*        ERRDLN      IFEQ 0
     C*                    Z-ADDOUTDIF    DIFDAY
     C*                    ELSE
     *                     ...
     C*                    ENDIF
     *
     *------------------------------------------------------------
     *
     *------------------------------------------------------------
     * Copy input modules
     *------------------------------------------------------------
     /COPY DATDS
     /COPY ERRDS
     /COPY PGMSDS
     /COPY RERDS
     /COPY STDCONST
     *
     *------------------------------------------------------------
     * Entry point
     *------------------------------------------------------------
     C         *ENTRY      PLIST
     C                     PARM           INCNT1 10
```

Figure 24.4 ZDATDIF Difference Between Dates, continued

```
 ... 1 ...+... 2 ...+... 3 ...+... 4 ...+... 5 ...+... 6 ...+... 7 ...+... 8

C                       PARM            INDAT1 60
C                       PARM            INCNT2 10
C                       PARM            INDAT2 60
C                       PARM            OUTDIF 50
C                       PARM            RERDS
 *
 *-------------------------------------------------------------
 * Mainline
 *-------------------------------------------------------------
 *
 * Check for required number of parameters
 *
C           PSPRMS      IFLT 5
C                       MOVE *ON         *INLR
C                       RETRN
C                       ENDIF
 *
 * Initialize variables
 *
C                       RESETERRDS
C                       Z-ADD6           ERRPRM
C                       Z-ADD0           OUTDIF
C                       Z-ADD0           WKUNV1 60
C                       Z-ADD0           WKUNV2 60
 *
 * Convert first date from YMD to Julian to Universal
 *
C                       MOVE INCNT1      DTCNTI
C                       MOVE INDAT1      DTDATI
C                       MOVE DTFYMD      DTFMTI
C                       MOVE DTFJUL      DTFMTO
C                       EXSR DATCVT
 *
C           DTERR       IFEQ *OFF
C                       MOVE DTVARO      DTVARI
C                       EXSR DATJ2U
C                       MOVELDTDATO      WKUNV1
C                       ENDIF
 *
 * Convert second date from YMD to Julian to Universal
 *
C           DTERR       IFEQ *OFF
C                       MOVE INCNT2      DTCNTI
C                       MOVE INDAT2      DTDATI
C                       MOVE DTFYMD      DTFMTI
C                       MOVE DTFJUL      DTFMTO
C                       EXSR DATCVT
C                       ENDIF
 *
C           DTERR       IFEQ *OFF
C                       MOVE DTVARO      DTVARI
C                       EXSR DATJ2U
```

Figure 24.4 ZDATDIF Difference Between Dates, continued

```
... 1 ...+... 2 ...+... 3 ...+... 4 ...+... 5 ...+... 6 ...+... 7 ...+... 8

C                     MOVELDTDATO   WKUNV1
C                     ENDIF
 *
 * Calculate difference between dates
 *
C         DTERR       IFEQ *OFF
C         WKUNV2      SUB  WKUNV1     OUTDIF
C                     ENDIF
 *
 * Set return error
 *
C                     EXSR RERSET
 *
C                     RETRN
 *
 *-----------------------------------------------------------
 * Copy calc modules
 *-----------------------------------------------------------
 /COPY DATCVT
 /COPY DATJ2U
 /COPY RERSET
```

Exponentiation in RPG

Chapter 25

With this RPG program, you can code most complex business calculations that require exponentiation.

As a rule, RPG's simple arithmetic operations can handle most situations. But every rule has its exceptions — as you know if you've tried using RPG to calculate compound interest, or the annual percentage yield on an investment, as defined by the U.S. Truth in Savings Act (TISA). Such calculations use exponentiation; and, unfortunately, RPG/400 doesn't have an EXP op-code. However, this chapter provides the CLCEXP program (Figure 25.1) to perform the same function. CLCEXP is provided here as a called program. If you absolutely must, you could modify it to be a /COPY module for better performance. However, as coded, it performs well for almost all purposes.

CLCEXP lets you quickly perform exponentiation in RPG, accurate to seven significant digits. You call CLCEXP with four parameters:

CLNBR   declares the number to be raised to a power.

CLPWR   declares the power applied to CLNBR.

CLEXP   declares the result returned by program CLCEXP.

CLERR   declares a logical variable used to return errors from the program. CLERR will be set on if integer truncation occurs.

You must declare the first three parameters as numeric variables of 15 digits with six decimal places. You declare the last parameter as a character variable of 1 byte.

Let's see how to use CLCEXP to calculate the annual percentage yield on savings, which is defined by the U.S. TISA as

$$\text{Yield} = (1+(\text{Interest}/\text{Principal}))**(365/\text{Days})-1$$

The following code snippet shows how to implement the yield formula in RPG:

```
C           INTRST    DIV  PRINC   CLNBR
C                     ADD  1       CLNBR
 *
C           365       DIV  DAYS    CLPWR
 *
C                     CALL 'CLCEXP'
C                     PARM         CLNBR   156
C                     PARM         CLPWR   156
C                     PARM         CLEXP   156
C                     PARM         CLERR   1
 *
C           CLERR     IFEQ *OFF
C           CLEXP     SUB  1       YIELD
C                     ELSE
C                     Z-ADDO       YIELD
C                     ENDIF
```

The yield formula is broken down into four simple steps. First, calculate parameter CLNBR (the number to raise to a power), as shown in the first two lines of code. Second, calculate parameter CLPWR (the power to raise the number), as shown in the third line. Third, call CLCEXP to raise the number in CLNBR to the power in CLPWR, as shown in the next several lines of code. And last, subtract 1 from the exponent returned by CLCEXP to get the annual percentage yield. Notice that, as always with RPG, you code the calculation from the innermost set of parentheses outward.

The limited size of RPG's numeric fields can limit CLCEXP's accuracy. Test CLCEXP output thoroughly with your financial algorithms to ensure the accuracy is acceptable.

Program CLCEXP has one limitation you need to keep in mind. Because of the limited size of numeric fields in RPG, the result returned by CLCEXP is accurate only to about seven significant digits. Although this degree of accuracy is fine for most purposes, it could pose problems with some formulae in financial applications.

To determine whether or not CLCEXP is accurate enough for your requirements, you should first check any calculation you want to use with it. For example, let's look at the formula for annual yield shown above. Interest of $136.99 for 100 days on a principal of $10,000 produces a yield of 0.050916, which is correct when rounded to four decimal places. Substituting 1 day or 365 days into the calculation produces results with the same degree of accuracy, so CLCEXP is fine for this sort of calculation.

However, CLCEXP may not be suitable for some other calculations. For example, the amount due on a loan subject to compound interest can be defined as

AmountDue = LoanAmount*((1+InterestRate)**Periods)

Let's look at the right side of the calculation, which produces the compound interest rate. Using CLCEXP, a rate of 20 percent over 25½ years produces a compound rate of 104.501315; the correct result, however, is 104.5014. The difference may not seem like much, but it would result in a rounding down of the amount due of 1 cent per 100 dollars of the loan amount.

CLCEXP is a powerful RPG ally for complex statistical applications, with acceptable performance and accuracy for most jobs. Remember, though, to test CLCEXP with your financial algorithms to ensure that its RPG-constrained accuracy is acceptable.

Figure 25.1 CLCEXP RPG Program

```
... 1 ...+... 2 ...+... 3 ...+... 4 ...+... 5 ...+... 6 ...+... 7 ...+... 8


 *------------------------------------------------------------------
 * CLCEXP - Calculate exponent of number raised to power
 *
 * Function:
 *   Calculates the exponent of a number raised to any power.
 *   Note: the number must be positive.
 *
 * Parameters:
 *   CLNBR   - calc_number
 *   CLPWR   - calc_power
 *   CLEXP   - calc_number
 *   CLERR   - calc_error (*ON if calc_exponent is truncated)
 *
 * Example:
 *   Raise 2 to the power of 3.5 and place the answer in RESULT.
 *
C*                      Z-ADD2          CLNBR
C*                      Z-ADD3.5        CLPWR
 *
C*                      CALL 'CLCEXP'
C*                      PARM            CLNBR  156
C*                      PARM            CLPWR  156
C*                      PARM            CLEXP  156
C*                      PARM            CLERR    1
 *
C*         CLERR        IFEQ *OFF
C*                      Z-ADDCLEXP      RESULT
C*                      ELSE
 *                      ...
C*                      ENDIF
 *
 *------------------------------------------------------------------
 *
 *------------------------------------------------------------------
 * Named constants
 *------------------------------------------------------------------
I                 -.69314718          C       LNHLF
I                 0.69314718          C       LN2
I                 2.30258509          C       LN10
I                 6.90775527          C       LN1000
 *
 *------------------------------------------------------------------
 * Copy input modules
```

Figure 25.1 CLCEXP RPG Program, continued

```
... 1 ...+... 2 ...+... 3 ...+... 4 ...+... 5 ...+... 6 ...+... 7 ...+... 8

     *-----------------------------------------------------------
     /COPY PGMSDS
     *
     *-----------------------------------------------------------
     * Entry point
     *-----------------------------------------------------------
     C           *ENTRY    PLIST
     C                     PARM           CLNBR   156
     C                     PARM           CLPWR   156
     C                     PARM           CLEXP   156
     C                     PARM           CLERR   1
     *
     *-----------------------------------------------------------
     * Mainline
     *-----------------------------------------------------------
     *
     * Check for required number of parameters
     *
     C           PSPRMS    IFLT 4
     C                     MOVE *ON        *INLR
     C                     RETRN
     C                     ENDIF
     *
     C                     Z-ADD0          CLEXP
     C                     MOVE *OFF       CLERR
     *
     * Check for power equal to 0
     *
     C           CLPWR     IFEQ 0
     C                     Z-ADD1          CLEXP
     C                     RETRN
     C                     ENDIF
     *
     * Check for number equal to 0 or 1
     *
     C           CLNBR     IFEQ 0
     C           CLNBR     OREQ 1
     C                     Z-ADDCLNBR      CLEXP
     C                     RETRN
     C                     ENDIF
     *
     * result = exp( ln( number ) * power )
     *
     C           CLNBR     IFGT 0
     C                     Z-ADDCLNBR      NUM
     C                     ELSE
     C                     Z-SUBCLNBR      NUM
     C                     ENDIF
     *
     C                     EXSR CLCLN
     *
     C           MTHERR    IFEQ *OFF
```

Figure 25.1 CLCEXP RPG Program, continued

```
    ... 1 ...+... 2 ...+... 3 ...+... 4 ...+... 5 ...+... 6 ...+... 7 ...+... 8

     *
    C                       MULT CLPWR      LN
    C                       EXSR CLCEXP
    C           CLNBR       IFGT 0
    C                       Z-ADDEXP        CLEXP
    C                       ELSE
    C                       Z-SUBEXP        CLEXP
    C                       ENDIF
     *
    C                       ENDIF
     *
    C                       MOVE MTHERR     CLERR
     *
    C                       RETRN
     *
     *------------------------------------------------------------------
     * CLCLN   - Calculates natural logarithm of number
     *
     * The natural logarithm of a number can be expressed by the
     * power series:
     *    ln x = (x-1) - ((x-1)**2)/2 + ((x-1)**3)/3 - ...
     *                                           (for 0 < x <= 2)
     *------------------------------------------------------------------
    C           CLCLN       BEGSR
     *
     * Declare global variables
     *
    C                       Z-ADDLN         LN     159
    C                       Z-ADDNUM        NUM    156
    C                       MOVE *OFF       MTHERR  1
     *
     * Declare local variables
     *
    C                       Z-ADD1          @INCR  159
    C                       Z-ADD0          @EXP2  159
    C                       Z-ADD0          @INT    70
    C                       Z-ADD0          @MANT  159
    C                       Z-ADD-1         @PWRN  159
    C                       Z-ADD0          @SUMM  159
     *
     * Number must be greater than 0
     *
    C           NUM         IFLE 0
    C                       MOVE *ON        MTHERR
    C                       GOTO ENDLN
    C                       ENDIF
     *
     * Convert number to mantissa and exponent in the range
     * (1 <= mantissa <= 1.34) to satisfy the limits of the
     * summation and improve performance.
     *
    C           NUM         IFLT 1000000
```

Figure 25.1 CLCEXP RPG Program, continued

```
... 1 ...+... 2 ...+... 3 ...+... 4 ...+... 5 ...+... 6 ...+... 7 ...+... 8

C                       Z-ADDNUM        @MANT
C                       ELSE
C                       MOVE NUM        @MANT
C                       Z-ADDLN1000     @EXP2
C                       ENDIF
 *
C          @MANT        DOWLT1
C                       MULT 10         @MANT
C                       SUB  LN10       @EXP2
C                       ENDDO
 *
C          @MANT        DOWGE10
C                       MULT 0.1        @MANT
C                       ADD  LN10       @EXP2
C                       ENDDO
 *
C          @MANT        DOWGE1.34
C                       MULT 0.5        @MANT
C                       ADD  LN2        @EXP2
C                       ENDDO
 *
 * Summate power series while increment is not 0
 *
C                       SUB  1          @MANT
 *
C          @INCR        DOWNE0
 *
C                       MULT @MANT      @PWRN
C                       Z-SUB@PWRN      @PWRN
C                       ADD  1          @INT
C          @PWRN        DIV  @INT       @INCR
C                       ADD  @INCR      @SUMM
 *
C                       ENDDO
 *
C          @SUMM        ADD  @EXP2      LN        H
 *
C          ENDLN        ENDSR
 *
 *-----------------------------------------------------------
 * CLCEXP - Calculates exponential of a natural logarithm
 *
 * The exponential of a natural logarithm can be expressed by
 * the power series:
 *   exp x = 1 + x + (x**2)/2! + (x**3)/3! + ...
 *         = 1 + x + (x)*(x/2) + (x)*(x/2)*(x/3) + ...
 *                                              (for all x)
 *-----------------------------------------------------------
C          CLCEXP       BEGSR
 *
 * Declare global variables
 *
```

Figure 25.1 CLCEXP RPG Program, continued

```
 ... 1 ...+... 2 ...+... 3 ...+... 4 ...+... 5 ...+... 6 ...+... 7 ...+... 8
C                        Z-ADDEXP        EXP    156
C                        Z-ADDLN         LN     159
C                        MOVE *OFF       MTHERR  1
 *
 * Declare local variables
 *
C                        Z-ADD1          @INCR  159
C                        Z-ADD1          @EXP   156
C                        Z-ADD0          @INT    70
C                        Z-ADD0          @INTMX 150
C                        Z-ADD0          @MANT  159
C                        Z-ADD1          @SUMM  159
 *
 * Convert number to mantissa and exponent in the range
 * (ln .5 <= mantissa <= 1) to increase the accuracy and
 * the performance of the summation.
 *
C                        Z-ADDLN         @MANT
 *
C           @MANT        DOWLTLNHLF
C                        ADD  LN10       @MANT
C                        MULT 0.1        @EXP
C                        ENDDO
 *
C           @MANT        DOWGT0
C                        SUB  LN10       @MANT
C                        MULT 10         @EXP
C                        ENDDO
 *
C           @MANT        DOWLTLNHLF
C                        ADD  LN2        @MANT
C                        MULT 0.5        @EXP
C                        ENDDO
 *
 * Summate power series while increment is not 0
 *
C           @INCR        DOWNE0
 *
C                        ADD  1          @INT
C                        MULT @MANT      @INCR
C                        DIV  @INT       @INCR
C                        ADD  @INCR      @SUMM
 *
C                        ENDDO
 *
C           @SUMM        MULT @EXP       EXP       H
 *
 * Check for integer truncation
 *
C           @SUMM        MULT @EXP       @INTMX
 *
C           EXP          IFLT @INTMX
```

Figure 25.1 CLCEXP RPG Program, continued

```
... 1 ...+... 2 ...+... 3 ...+... 4 ...+... 5 ...+... 6 ...+... 7 ...+... 8

C           @EXP      OREQ 0
C                     MOVE @ON     MTHERR
C                     END
  *
C                     ENDSR
```

Using User Spaces

Chapter 26

Use these modules to simplify working with user spaces in your programs.

A user space is an object used to store temporary data required by a program. User spaces are not organized by records and fields; rather, they are a contiguous stream of bytes with no implicit organization. A user space's storage organization is a bit like that of a data area; however, where a data area can be a maximum of 2,000 bytes, a user space can be up to a whoppin' 16 MB.

IBM list APIs, such as the List Objects API (QUSLOBJ), direct their output to a user space that you can process in an RPG program. User spaces also provide a fast and efficient means for storing large amounts of application data required by your programs. In this chapter, we cover the four basic steps you need to understand for working with user spaces: create, change, retrieve, and delete. In the next chapter, we will look at how to retrieve the information generated by IBM list APIs.

The /COPY modules included in this chapter are

USDS	provides the USDS user space data structures required by the following members (Figure 26.1).
USCRT	creates a user space (Figure 26.2).
USCHG	changes the contents of a user space (Figure 26.3).
USRTV	retrieves the contents of a user space (Figure 26.4).
USDLT	deletes a user space (Figure 26.5).

You will also need the ERRDS module shown in Figure 2.2 (Chapter 2).

To use the modules, you include the ERRDS and USDS data structures at the end of the I-specs. The remaining four modules include subroutines for performing user space functions, and they should be included at the end of the C-specs. We normally stick to the convention of coding a single subroutine in each C-spec copy module, and of using the same name for both the subroutine and the module. So the USCRT member contains subroutine USCRT, USCHG contains subroutine USCHG, and so on. Each subroutine uses the ERRDS data structure to provide feedback about runtime errors. After executing each of the subroutines provided, to test for errors you must check the ERRDLN field (which is returned in the ERRDS data structure after each call to a user-space API).

```
C           ERRDLN      IFNE 0
  :                       handle error here
C                       ENDIF
```

To create a user space, you use the USCRT subroutine, specifying the name and library of the user space and its size. To create a user space of 8,000 bytes called INVUS in library QTEMP, you code

```
C                       MOVEL'INVUS'  USNAM      P
C                       MOVEL'QTEMP'  USLIB      P
C                       Z-ADD8000     USSIZ
C                       EXSR USCRT
C           ERRDLN      IFNE 0
  :                       handle error here
C                       ENDIF
```

Once you have created a user space, you can change or retrieve its contents as often as you want. To change the contents of a user space, you use the USCHG subroutine, specifying a pointer to the starting position you want to change, the length of the data, and the data itself. To store the contents of an INVDS data structure of 80 bytes, starting in position 1 of the INVUS user space, you code

```
C                       MOVEL'INVUS'  USNAM      P
C                       MOVEL'QTEMP'  USLIB      P
C                       Z-ADD1        USPTR
C                       Z-ADD80       USLEN
C                       MOVELINVDS    UDDS       P
C                       EXSR USCHG
C           ERRDLN      IFNE 0
  :                       handle error here
C                       ENDIF
```

You use the USRTV subroutine to retrieve the contents of a user space. Just as with USCHG, USRTV needs to know the position and length of the data, and it requires a variable to store the data returned from the user space:

```
C                         MOVEL'INVUS'    USNAM      P
C                         MOVEL'QTEMP'    USLIB      P
C                         Z-ADD1          USPTR
C                         Z-ADD80         USLEN
C                         EXSR USRTV
C           ERRDLN        IFNE 0
  :                       handle error here
C                         ELSE
C                         MOVELIUDDS      INVDS      P
C                         ENDIF
```

Finally, to delete a user space, you use the USDLT subroutine, specifying the name and library of the user space:

```
C                         MOVEL'INVUS'    USNAM      P
C                         MOVEL'QTEMP'    USLIB      P
C                         EXSR USDLT
C           ERRDLN        IFNE 0
  :                       handle error here
C                         ENDIF
```

The copy modules simplify the code required to work with user spaces, but how and when should you use them? As we said earlier, user spaces are ideal for storing large amounts of application data required by a program. For example, consider a job that posts a batch of inventory transactions. Each transaction could contain many detail lines. The job may have to validate each transaction and reject any transaction that has any line in error. This type of processing requires two passes of the data — one for error checking, and one for posting. Instead of performing two sets of random I/O on the data, or using work files, you can store a complete transaction in a user space and then retrieve it once for each pass.

Also note that user spaces can be shared among programs, so you can store the data in one program and then pass the name of the user space, together with its current size, to separate subprograms for validity checking and posting. This capability improves the modularity of your code with very little impact on performance.

Figure 26.1 USDS User Space Data Structure

```
... 1 ...+... 2 ...+... 3 ...+... 4 ...+... 5 ...+... 6 ...+... 7 ...+... 8

*-------------------------------------------------------------------
* USDS - Data structures for User Space functions
*
* Function:
*   Defines data structures for User Space functions.
*
* USDS   - user_space_DS:
*   USQNAM - user_space_qual_name
*     USNAM  - user_space_name
*     USLIB  - user_space_lib
```

Figure 26.1 USDS User Space Data Structure, continued

```
... 1 ...+... 2 ...+... 3 ...+... 4 ...+... 5 ...+... 6 ...+... 7 ...+... 8

     *    USATR  - user_space_attr
     *    USSIZ  - user_space_initial_size
     *    USVAL  - user_space_initial_value
     *    USAUT  - user_space_authority
     *    USTXT  - user_space_text_desc
     *    USRPL  - user_space_replace
     *    USPTR  - user_space_data_ptr
     *    USLEN  - user_space_data_len
     *    USDTA  - user_space_data
     *-----------------------------------------------------------------
    IUSDS      IDS
    I                                        1   20 USQNAM
    I                                        1   10 USNAM
    I                                       11   20 USLIB
     *
    I                                       21   30 USATR
    I                                   B   31  340USSIZ
    I                                       35   35 USVAL
    I I              '*CHANGE'              36   45 USAUT
    I                                       46   95 USTXT
    I I              '*YES'                 96  105 USRPL
     *
    I                                   B  106 1090USPTR
    I                                   B  110 1130USLEN
     *
     *-----------------------------------------------------------------
     * UDDS   - user_space_data_DS
     *-----------------------------------------------------------------
    IUDDS      IDS                            9999
```

Figure 26.2 USCRT Create User Space Function

```
... 1 ...+... 2 ...+... 3 ...+... 4 ...+... 5 ...+... 6 ...+... 7 ...+... 8

     *-----------------------------------------------------------------
     * USCRT - Create User Space function
     *
     * Function:
     *   Create a user space. Note: only IBM list APIs can extend
     *   the size of a user space, so take care in specifying the
     *   size of all other user spaces.
     *
     * Requires copy modules:
     *   USDS   - Data structures for User Space functions
     *
     * Expects:
     *   USQNAM - user_space_qual_name:
     *     USNAM  - user_space_name
     *     USLIB  - user_space_lib
     *   USSIZ  - user_space_initial_size
     *
     * Returns:
```

Figure 26.2 USCRT Create User Space Function, continued

```
... 1 ...+... 2 ...+... 3 ...+... 4 ...+... 5 ...+... 6 ...+... 7 ...+... 8

*    USQNAM - user_space_qual_name
*    ERRDS  - err_API_DS
*
* Example:
*    Create a user space called MYSPC in MYLIB with a size
*    of 8000 bytes, and save the qualified name in MYUS.
*
C*               MOVEL'MYSPC'  USNAM    P
C*               MOVEL'MYLIB'  USLIB    P
C*               Z-ADD8000     USSIZ
C*               EXSR USCRT
 *
C*       ERRDLN  IFNE 0
C*               MOVELUSQNAM   MYUS
C*               ELSE
 *               ...
C*               ENDIF
 *
*------------------------------------------------------------------
C        USCRT   BEGSR
 *
C                CALL 'QUSCRTUS'
C                PARM          USQNAM
C                PARM          USATR
C                PARM          USSIZ
C                PARM          USVAL
C                PARM          USAUT
C                PARM          USTXT
C                PARM          USRPL
C                PARM          ERRDS
 *
C                ENDSR
```

Figure 26.3 USCHG Change User Space Function

```
... 1 ...+... 2 ...+... 3 ...+... 4 ...+... 5 ...+... 6 ...+... 7 ...+... 8

*------------------------------------------------------------------
* USCHG - Change User Space function
*
* Function:
*    Changes the contents of part of an existing user space.
*
* Requires copy modules:
*    USDS   - Data structures for User Space functions
*
* Expects:
*    USQNAM - user_space_qual_name:
*      USNAM  - user_space_name
*      USLIB  - user_space_lib
*    USPTR  - user_space_data_ptr
*    USLEN  - user_space_data_len
```

Figure 26.3 USCHG Change User Space Function, continued

```
... 1 ...+... 2 ...+... 3 ...+... 4 ...+... 5 ...+... 6 ...+... 7 ...+... 8

     *    UDDS    - user_space_data_DS
     *
     * Returns:
     *   ERRDS   - err_API_DS
     *
     * Example:
     *   Replace the first 80 characters of a user space called
     *   MYSPC in library MYLIB with the contents of the field DATA.
     *
    C*                    MOVEL'MYSPC'   USNAM    P
    C*                    MOVEL'MYLIB'   USLIB    P
    C*                    Z-ADD1         USPTR
    C*                    Z-ADD80        USLEN
    C*                    MOVELDATA      UDDS     P
    C*                    EXSR USCHG
     *
    C*        ERRDLN     IFNE 0
     *                    ...
    C*                    ENDIF
     *
     *----------------------------------------------------------------
    C         USCHG      BEGSR
     *
    C                    CALL 'QUSCHGUS'
    C                    PARM           USQNAM
    C                    PARM           USPTR
    C                    PARM           USLEN
    C                    PARM           UDDS
     * Note: The following line specifies a zero, not the letter O.
    C                    PARM '0'       US@CHG   1
    C                    PARM           ERRDS
     *
    C                    ENDSR
```

Figure 26.4 USRTV Retrieve User Space Function

```
... 1 ...+... 2 ...+... 3 ...+... 4 ...+... 5 ...+... 6 ...+... 7 ...+... 8

     *----------------------------------------------------------------
     * USRTV - Retrieve User Space function
     *
     * Function:
     *   Retrieves the contents of part of an existing user space.
     *
     * Requires copy modules:
     *   USDS    - Data structures for User Space functions
     *
     * Expects:
     *   USQNAM - user_space_qual_name:
     *     USNAM  - user_space_name
     *     USLIB  - user_space_lib
     *   USPTR  - user_space_data_ptr
```

Figure 26.4 USRTV Retrieve User Space Function, continued

```
... 1 ...+... 2 ...+... 3 ...+... 4 ...+... 5 ...+... 6 ...+... 7 ...+... 8

     *    USLEN  - user_space_data_len
     *
     * Returns:
     *    UDDS   - user_space_data_DS
     *    ERRDS  - err_API_DS
     *
     * Example:
     *    Retrieve the first 80 characters of a user space called
     *    MYSPC in library MYLIB into the field DATA.
     *
     C*                        MOVEL'MYSPC'   USNAM     P
     C*                        MOVEL'MYLIB'   USLIB     P
     C*                        Z-ADD1         USPTR
     C*                        Z-ADD80        USLEN
     C*                        EXSR USRTV
     *
     C*          ERRDLN        IFEQ 0
     C*                        MOVELUDDS      DATA      P
     C*                        ELSE
     *                         ...
     C*                        ENDIF
     *
     *-------------------------------------------------------------------
     C           USRTV         BEGSR
     *
     C                         CALL 'QUSRTVUS'
     C                         PARM           USQNAM
     C                         PARM           USPTR
     C                         PARM           USLEN
     C                         PARM           UDDS
     C                         PARM           ERRDS
     *
     C                         ENDSR
```

Figure 26.5 USDLT Delete User Space Function

```
... 1 ...+... 2 ...+... 3 ...+... 4 ...+... 5 ...+... 6 ...+... 7 ...+... 8

     *-------------------------------------------------------------------
     * USDLT - Delete User Space function
     *
     * Function:
     *    Deletes an existing user space.
     *
     * Requires copy modules:
     *    USDS   - Data structures for User Space functions
     *
     * Expects:
     *    USQNAM - user_space_qual_name:
     *      USNAM  - user_space_name
     *      USLIB  - user_space_lib
     *
```

Figure 26.5 USDLT Delete User Space Function, continued

```
... 1 ...+... 2 ...+... 3 ...+... 4 ...+... 5 ...+... 6 ...+... 7 ...+... 8

 * Returns:
 *   ERRDS  - err_API_DS
 *
 * Example:
 *   Delete a user space called MYSPC in MYLIB.
 *
C*                      MOVEL'MYSPC'  USNAM    P
C*                      MOVEL'MYLIB'  USLIB    P
C*                      EXSR USDLT
 *
C*          ERRDLN     IFNE 0
 *                     ...
C*                     ENDIF
 *
 *----------------------------------------------------------------
C           USDLT      BEGSR
 *
C                      CALL 'QUSDLTUS'
C                      PARM           USQNAM
C                      PARM           ERRDS
 *
C                      ENDSR
```

Using List APIs

Chapter 27

Use these modules for easy access to the information returned by OS/400 list APIs.

The OS/400-provided list APIs are powerful tools for retrieving information about various types of objects on the AS/400. You can use the APIs to write programming tools that display or perform actions on lists of objects. Each list API outputs information to a user space in a common format to simplify the retrieval of entries from the list. A user space created by a list API contains a number of sections, the most important of which are a generic header that includes pointers to the list data, and the actual list entries. These sections of information are unique to each API and are documented in the *System API Reference* manual (SC41-3801).

In this chapter, we provide routines to access the entries returned by any list API, using the List Object API (QUSLOBJ) as an example. The /COPY modules included in this chapter are

OBJLDS	includes data structures required to list objects (Figure 27.1).
OBJLST	lists objects (Figure 27.2).
ULDS	includes data structures required to retrieve the list entries in a user space (Figure 27.3).
ULHRTV	retrieves the list header from a user space (Figure 27.4).
ULERTV	retrieves a list entry from a user space (Figure 27.5).

You will also need the modules described in the previous chapter on "Using User Spaces" to create and delete user spaces.

Although we refer to many copy modules in this chapter, very little specific code is required to use them. In addition to what you learned about user spaces in Chapter 26, you need only four short sections of code to process an object list. First, you code the copy statements for the required modules, putting these four copy statements at the end of your RPG program's I-specifications:

```
/COPY ERRDS
/COPY OBJLDS
/COPY ULDS
/COPY USDS
```

and putting the following five copy statements at the end of your RPG
program's C-specifications:

```
/COPY OBJLST
/COPY ULERTV
/COPY ULHRTV
/COPY USCRT
/COPY USDLT
```

Then, to use the QUSLOBJ API, you create a user space and use the
OBJLST subroutine, which writes a list of objects to the user space. To
output a detailed list of all inventory files in library APPLIB to a user
space called OBJUS in QTEMP, you code

```
    * Create a 50,000 byte user space
C                          MOVEL'OBJUS'    USNAM     P
C                          MOVEL'QTEMP'    USLIB     P
C                          Z-ADD500000     USSIZ
C                          EXSR USCRT
    *
    * Call the QUSLOBJ API to list all the *FILE
    * objects in the APPLIB with names that start
    * with INV.
C                          MOVEL'OBJUS'    USNAM     P
C                          MOVEL'QTEMP'    USLIB     P
C                          MOVE OL2FMT     ULFMT
C                          MOVEL'APPLIB'   OLLIB     P
C                          MOVEL'INV*'     OLOBJ     P
C                          MOVEL'*FILE'    OLTYP     P
C                          EXSR OBJLST
```

You'll notice we've sized the user space fairly large — at 50,000
bytes. Although list APIs automatically extend a user space when it
becomes full, extents are very slow; so it's a good idea to create a large
user space to keep extents to a minimum.

After the program performs the code above, the user space contains
the list of files found and — as all user spaces do — a generic user space
header that provides details (e.g., list length and number of list entries)
about the list information retrieved. Now all you have to do is traverse
through the user space, reading each entry. To do this, you first use
subroutine ULHRTV to retrieve the generic header for the user space:

```
      * Initialize list variables for routine ULHRTV
C               *LIKE      DEFN ULEPTR      OLEPTR
C               *LIKE      DEFN ULESIZ      OLESIZ
C               *LIKE      DEFN ULEOCR      OLEOCR
      *
      * Specify the user space to read
C                          MOVEL'OBJUS'     USNAM       P
C                          MOVEL'QTEMP'     USLIB       P
      * Read the user space header
C                          EXSR ULHRTV
C                          Z-ADDULEPTR      OLEPTR
C                          Z-ADDULESIZ      OLESIZ
C                          Z-ADDULEOCR      OLEOCR
```

Three fields are used to store the values we need to process the entries in the list: OLEPTR points to the first entry in the list, OLESIZ defines the size of each entry, OLEOCR defines the number of occurrences of the list. Routine ULHRTV retrieves this information from the user space header.

Finally, you use the ULERTV subroutine in conjunction with the three fields returned from the generic header to retrieve each entry in the list:

```
C               *LIKE      DEFN OLEOCR      OLEIDX
      *
      * For every entry in the list, do...
C               1          DO   OLEOCR      OLEIDX
C                          MOVEL'OBJUS'     USNAM       P
C                          MOVEL'QTEMP'     USLIB       P
C                          Z-ADDOLEPTR      ULEPTR
C                          Z-ADDOLESIZ      ULESIZ
      * Retrieve an entry putting the information
      * retrieved in the OBJDS data structure (shown in
      * Figure 27.1)
C                          EXSR ULERTV
C                          MOVELUDDS        OBJDS
C                          Z-ADDULEPTR      OLEPTR
C      :                   process entry
C                          ENDDO
```

On each iteration of the loop, a list entry is retrieved and moved to OBJDS for processing, and OLEPTR is updated to point to the next entry in the loop.

You may wonder why we bother copying the fields ULEPTR, ULESIZ, and ULECUR to their OLExxx counterparts, when we could just pass the ULExxx fields from subroutine ULHRTV to ULERTV. The reason is twofold. First, using two sets of fields makes the code snippets above more readable by showing the dependencies between the two subroutines. Second, the code is easier to extend. For example, we could use the Retrieve Member List API to list the members in each file returned by the List Object API without risk of the ULExxx fields for the member list corrupting those for the object list. It's well worth the trouble to pay attention to such minor details when you code, because doing so makes your programs easier to enhance.

A thorough discussion of user spaces and using the list APIs is beyond the scope of this book. However, the code provided in Chapter 26 and in this chapter, and an hour or two spent with the *System API Reference* manual, should make using the list APIs much easier for you.

Figure 27.1 OBJLDS Object List Data Structure

```
... 1 ...+... 2 ...+... 3 ...+... 4 ...+... 5 ...+... 6 ...+... 7 ...+... 8

   *-------------------------------------------------------------
   * OBJLDS - Data structure for Object List function
   *
   * Function:
   *   Defines the data structure for the entries created by the
   *   List Object function, OBJLST. Supports format 1 (basic data)
   *   and format 2 (descriptive data).
   *
   * OBJDS - obj_list_DS:
   *   Format 1:
   *      OLOBJ  - obj_list_obj
   *      OLLIB  - obj_list_lib
   *      OLTYP  - obj_list_obj_type
   *   Format 2:
   *      OLSTS  - obj_list_status
   *      OLATR  - obj_list_attr
   *      OLTXT  - obj_list_text_desc
   *      OLUATR - obj_list_user_attr
   *      OL102  - obj_list_filler_102
   *-------------------------------------------------------------
IOBJDS     IDS
I                                        1  10 OLOBJ
I                                       11  20 OLLIB
I                                       21  30 OLTYP
   *
I                                       31  31 OLSTS
I                                       32  41 OLATR
I                                       42  91 OLTXT
I                                       92 101 OLUATR
I                                      102 108 OL102
   *
   *-------------------------------------------------------------
   *   OL1FMT - obj_list1_fmt
   *   OL2FMT - obj_list2_fmt
   *-------------------------------------------------------------
I              'OBJL0100'             C       OL1FMT
I              'OBJL0200'             C       OL2FMT
```

Figure 27.2 OBJLST Object List Function

```
 ... 1 ...+... 2 ...+... 3 ...+... 4 ...+... 5 ...+... 6 ...+... 7 ...+... 8


  *-----------------------------------------------------------------
  * OBJLST - List objects function
  *
  * Function:
  *   Creates a list of objects of a type in a library. The list
  *   is stored in a user space. Use the USCRT function to create
  *   the user space. Use the ULHRTV function to retrieve the
  *   list header, and the ULERTV function to retrieve the list
  *   entries.
  *
  * Requires copy modules:
  *   OBJLDS - Data structure for Object List function
  *   USDS   - Data structures for User Space functions
  *   ULDS   - Data structure for User Space List functions
  *
  * Expects:
  *   USQNAM - user_space_qual_name:
  *     USNAM  - user_space_name
  *     USLIB  - user_space_lib
  *   ULFMT  - user_space_API_format of:
  *     OL1FMT - obj_list1_fmt
  *     OL2FMT - obj_list2_fmt
  *   OLOBJ  - obj_list_obj or generic object or *ALL
  *   OLLIB  - obj_list_lib or *ALL or *ALLUSR or *CURLIB
  *                       or *LIBL or *USRLIBL
  *   OLTYP  - obj_list_type
  *
  * Returns:
  *   ERRDS  - err_API_DS
  *
  * Example:
  *   Output a list of objects with the generic name INV* of
  *   type *FILE in library APPLIB to the user space MYSPC
  *   in library MYLIB. The list contains the format 2
  *   information OL2FMT for each object.
  *
C*                    MOVEL'MYSPC'    USNAM       P
C*                    MOVEL'MYLIB'    USLIB       P
C*                    MOVE OL2FMT     ULFMT
C*                    MOVEL'APPLIB'   OLLIB       P
C*                    MOVEL'INV*'     OLOBJ       P
C*                    MOVEL'*FILE'    OLTYP       P
C*                    EXSR OBJLST
  *
  *-----------------------------------------------------------------
C           OBJLST    BEGSR
  *
C                     MOVELOLOBJ      OL@QNM
C                     MOVE OLLIB      OL@QNM
C                     MOVE OLTYP      OL@TYP
```

Figure 27.2 OBJLST Object List Function, continued

```
... 1 ...+... 2 ...+... 3 ...+... 4 ...+... 5 ...+... 6 ...+... 7 ...+... 8

 *
C                     CALL 'QUSLOBJ'
C                     PARM          USQNAM
C                     PARM          ULFMT
C                     PARM          OL@QNM 20
C                     PARM          OL@TYP 10
C                     PARM          ERRDS
 *
C                     ENDSR
```

Figure 27.3 ULDS User Space List Data Structure

```
... 1 ...+... 2 ...+... 3 ...+... 4 ...+... 5 ...+... 6 ...+... 7 ...+... 8

 *-----------------------------------------------------------------
 * ULDS - Data structure for User Space List functions
 *
 * Function:
 *   Defines the data structure for the list header information
 *   in a user space created by an IBM compatible List API.
 *   Use the ULHRTV function to retrieve the data structure.
 *
 * ULDS    - user_space_list_header_DS:
 *   ULARA  - user_space_user_area
 *   ULGSIZ - user_space_generic_header_size
 *   ULRLS  - user_space_release_level
 *   ULFMT  - user_space_API_format
 *   ULAPI  - user_space_API_name
 *   ULDTM  - user_space_data_time_stamp
 *   ULSTS  - user_space_status (Complete, Incomplete, Partial)
 *   ULSIZ  - user_space_size
 *   ULPOFF - user_space_parm_offset
 *   ULPSIZ - user_space_parm_size
 *   ULHOFF - user_space_header_offset
 *   ULHSIZ - user_space_header_size
 *   ULLOFF - user_space_list_offset
 *   ULLSIZ - user_space_list_size
 *   ULEOCR - user_space_entry_occurs
 *   ULESIZ - user_space_entry_size
 *-----------------------------------------------------------------
IULDS       IDS
I                                      1   64 ULARA
I                                    B 65  680ULGSIZ
I                                     69   72 ULRLS
I                                     73   80 ULFMT
I                                     81   90 ULAPI
I                                     91  103 ULDTM
I                                    104  104 ULSTS
I                                    B 105 1080ULSIZ
I                                    B 109 1120ULPOFF
I                                    B 113 1160ULPSIZ
I                                    B 117 1200ULHOFF
```

Figure 27.3 ULDS User Space List Data Structure, continued

```
... 1 ...+... 2 ...+... 3 ...+... 4 ...+... 5 ...+... 6 ...+... 7 ...+... 8

I                                      B 121 1240ULHSIZ
I                                      B 125 1280ULLOFF
I                                      B 129 1320ULLSIZ
I                                      B 133 1360ULEOCR
I                                      B 137 1400ULESIZ
 *
 *-----------------------------------------------------------------
 *   ULHPTR - user_space_header_ptr
 *   ULHLEN - user_space_header_len
 *-----------------------------------------------------------------
I            1                      C        ULHPTR
I            140                    C        ULHLEN
```

Figure 27.4 ULHRTV Retrieve User Space List Header

```
... 1 ...+... 2 ...+... 3 ...+... 4 ...+... 5 ...+... 6 ...+... 7 ...+... 8

 *-----------------------------------------------------------------
 * ULHRTV - Retrieve User Space List Header function
 *
 * Function:
 *   Retrieves the list header from a user space created by an
 *   IBM compatible List API. Use the USCRT function to create
 *   the user space, and a List API to load it. Use the ULERTV
 *   function to retrieve the list entries after running this
 *   function.
 *
 * Requires copy modules:
 *   ULDS    - Data structure for User Space List functions
 *   USDS    - Data structures for User Space functions
 *
 * Expects:
 *   USQNAM - user_space_qual_name:
 *     USNAM  - user_space_name
 *     USLIB  - user_space_lib
 *
 * Returns:
 *   ULDS    - user_space_list_header_DS, including:
 *     ULEOCR - user_space_entry_occurs
 *     ULESIZ - user_space_entry_size
 *   ULEPTR - user_space_entry_ptr (to first entry)
 *   ERRDS  - err_API_DS
 *
 * Example:
 *   Retrieve the list header for the user space MYSPC in
 *   library MYLIB. The function returns the following data
 *   for input to Retrieve User Space List Entry function
 *   RTVULE: MLEPTR points to the first list entry; MLESIZ
 *   is the size of an entry; MLEOCR is the number of
 *   occurrences in the list.
 *
C*                        MOVEL'MYSPC'  USNAM      P
```

Figure 27.4 ULHRTV Retrieve User Space List Header, continued

```
... 1 ...+... 2 ...+... 3 ...+... 4 ...+... 5 ...+... 6 ...+... 7 ...+... 8

C*                    MOVEL'MYLIB'   USLIB      P
C*                    EXSR ULHRTV
C*                    Z-ADDULEPTR    MLEPTR
C*                    Z-ADDULESIZ    MLESIZ
C*                    Z-ADDULEOCR    MLEOCR
 *
 *----------------------------------------------------------------
C          ULHRTV     BEGSR
 *
C          *LIKE      DEFN ULLOFF    ULEPTR
 *
C                     Z-ADDULHPTR    USPTR
C                     Z-ADDULHLEN    USLEN
 *
C                     CALL 'QUSRTVUS'
C                     PARM           USQNAM
C                     PARM           USPTR
C                     PARM           USLEN
C                     PARM           ULDS
C                     PARM           ERRDS
 *
C          ULLOFF     ADD  1         ULEPTR
 *
C                     ENDSR
```

Figure 27.5 ULERTV Retrieve User Space List Entry Function

```
... 1 ...+... 2 ...+... 3 ...+... 4 ...+... 5 ...+... 6 ...+... 7 ...+... 8

 *----------------------------------------------------------------
 * ULERTV - Retrieve User Space List Entry function
 *
 * Function:
 *   Retrieves an entry from a user space created by an IBM
 *   compatible List API. Use the USCRT function to create the
 *   user space, and a List API to load it. Use the ULHRTV
 *   function to retrieve the user space list header before
 *   using this function to retrieve the list entries.
 *
 * Requires copy modules:
 *   ULDS    - Data structure for User Space List functions
 *   USDS    - Data structures for User Space functions
 *
 * Expects:
 *   USQNAM - user_space_qual_name:
 *     USNAM  - user_space_name
 *     USLIB  - user_space_lib
 *   ULESIZ - user_space_entry_size
 *   ULEPTR - user_space_entry_ptr (to current entry)
 *
 * Returns:
 *   UDDS    - user_space_data_DS
```

Figure 27.5 ULERTV Retrieve User Space List Entry Function, continued

```
... 1 ...+... 2 ...+... 3 ...+... 4 ...+... 5 ...+... 6 ...+... 7 ...+... 8

     *    ULEPTR - user_space_entry_ptr (to next entry)
     *    ERRDS  - err_API_DS
     *
     * Example:
     *    Retrieve the entries from the user space MYSPC in library
     *    MYLIB and move them to the member description data
     *    structure MDDS for processing. Uses the following data
     *    returned by RTVULH: MLEPTR points to the next list entry;
     *    MLESIZ is the size of an entry; MLEOCR is the number of
     *    occurrences in the list.
     *
C*              1          DO    MLEOCR    MLEIDX
     *
C*                         MOVEL'MYSPC'    USNAM     P
C*                         MOVEL'MYLIB'    USLIB     P
C*                         Z-ADDMLEPTR     ULEPTR
C*                         Z-ADDMLESIZ     ULESIZ
C*                         EXSR ULERTV
C*                         MOVELUDDS       MLDS
C*                         Z-ADDULEPTR     MLEPTR
     *                     ...
C*                         ENDDO
     *
     *-----------------------------------------------------------------
C               ULERTV     BEGSR
     *
C                          Z-ADDULEPTR     USPTR
C                          Z-ADDULESIZ     USLEN
     *
C                          CALL 'QUSRTVUS'
C                          PARM            USQNAM
C                          PARM            USPTR
C                          PARM            USLEN
C                          PARM            UDDS
C                          PARM            ERRDS
     *
C                          ADD  ULESIZ     ULEPTR
     *
C                          ENDSR
```

File Maintenance
Without Record Locks

Chapter 28

Use the following technique to write safe and robust file maintenance programs that don't lock records while they are displayed to the user.

Perhaps owing to legacy RPG limitations (i.e., its previous inability to read an unlocked record from an update file), many RPG maintenance programs always lock a record while it is displayed for the user to change. The up side is that data integrity is preserved because no other job on the system can change the locked record. The down side is that any other job trying to update the record must wait until it is released. Real problems arise when the "other" job is a critical batch update that bombs because the wait-for-file value on the file's description is reached and the job terminates abnormally. In this chapter we show you an alternative approach to maintaining files that keeps the up side and gets rid of the down side. The technique, reading files with No Intention To Update, is called NITU for short.

With the NITU approach, three buffers are used to store the entire contents of any record that needs updating. One buffer is used to store a "snapshot" of the record before the operator makes changes, one buffer is used to save a snapshot of the the operator's changes, and a third buffer contains the record contents as it is read from disk a second time. The following pseudocode shows NITU in action:

```
Read unlocked Record A into CurrentBuffer
OldBuffer = CurrentBuffer
Make changes as needed to CurrentBuffer
NewBuffer = CurrentBuffer
Reread locked Record A into CurrentBuffer
If Record A deleted then
  Display record deleted message
Else
If CurrentBuffer <> OldBuffer then
  Display record changed since first read message
  Unlock Record A
```

```
     Else
       Update Record A with NewBuffer contents
     EndIf
```

If another job has updated the record, you treat the user's changes as an error, and display a message to that effect. You could add logic to the algorithm to enable the user to press F5 to refresh the data displayed and rekey his or her changes to the new version displayed.

Let's look at how to apply the NITU pseudocode to RPG in a typical file maintenance program. The program maintains an Item Master file (ITMMST), with record format ITMMSTR, keyed on item number (IMITM). The F-specs define ITMMST as an update file:

```
FITMMST  UF  E              K        DISK                          A
```

The I-specs include three data structures to store copies of the INVMSTR record format:

```
IEDTDS      EIDSITMMST                    9999
IOLDDS      IDS                           9999
INEWDS      IDS                           9999
```

The EDTDS data structure uses the external definition of the INVMST file to store the data from a record. The OLDDS and NEWDS data structures are used as temporary storage areas for a record. (From our pseudocode, EDTDS corresponds to the CurrentBuffer, OLDDS corresponds to the OldBuffer, and NEWDS corresponds to the NewBuffer). Note how all the data structures are defined as 9,999 bytes long, rather than with the actual record length of the INVMST file. This buffer length independence is so that the program can simply be recompiled if new fields are added to the file.

When a record is selected for maintenance, it is read with no-lock specified on the CHAIN operation (by putting an N in column 53), and the contents of the file are saved to the OLDDS data structure:

```
     * Read record to update with no lock
     C          IMKEY     CHAINITMMST                   N99
     * Save current record contents to OldBuffer
     C                    MOVE EDTDS     OLDDS
```

The contents of the record are then displayed for the user to change.

After the user makes any changes and presses Enter, the data is then validated as normal. If no errors occur with the new field values, the following code is executed:

```
* Field values have been validated, attempt update
*
* Save modified field values to NewBuffer
C                       MOVE EDTDS     NEWDS
* Reread record with lock this time
C          IMKEY        CHAINITMMST                 99
*
C                       SELEC
*
C          *IN99        WHEQ *ON
* Display record deleted message
   :
C          EDTDS        WHNE OLDDS
* Display record changed since first read message
   :
C                       UNLCKITMMST
* Put modified values back in CurrentBuffer
* (perhaps to redisplay to the user)
C                       MOVE NEWDS     EDTDS
   :
C                       OTHER
* Update record with NewBuffer contents
C                       MOVE NEWDS     EDTDS
C                       UPDATITMMSTR
   :
C                       ENDSL
```

The data returned from the display file is saved to the NEWDS data structure. The INVMST record is then read and locked. If the record is not found, then another job has deleted it. If the record just read (in EDTDS) is different from the one displayed (in OLDDS), then another job has changed it; so the record is unlocked and the user's changes in NEWDS are restored to EDTDS. When no errors are found, the user's changes are restored and the record updated.

You can use the code snippet above as the basis for checking additions and deletions. For an addition, if the record already exists, it has been added by another job, and the current record must be unlocked and an error displayed. For a deletion, if the record no longer exists, it has been deleted by another job, and an error message should be displayed. With additional buffers, this technique also can easily be adapted to applications that update records from more than one file with each display screen.

As you can see, the NITU technique requires very little coding and can greatly improve the robustness of your file maintenance programs. The code's simplicity is due primarily to RPG's ability to compare or move entire data structures with a single operation. This is a powerful feature of RPG for which you will find many other uses.

Getting the Most from /COPY

Appendix A

Much of this book's code is presented as /COPY modules. This appendix outlines a strategy for using /COPY modules in your production code.

Many RPG programs contain duplicate code. When it's not practical to split the duplicate code into a called program, move it to a separate member you can include in your programs at compilation using RPG's /COPY statement.

The /COPY statement is coded from position 7 of a source line and has the following format:

```
/COPY SRCLIB/SRCFIL,MBR
```

Both the source library and file are optional, allowing you to code just the member name:

```
/COPY MBR
```

When only the member name is specified, the RPG compiler searches all QRPGSRC source files in your library list to locate the member. This shorthand approach is very powerful, because the /COPY statement is not bound to a specific file and library. You can change the entries in your library list to compile programs with different versions of copy members for testing. You can also use QRPGSRC in different libraries for different types of copy members. For example, QRPGSRC in GENLIB might contain general routines you can use in any program, while QRPGSRC in INVLIB might contain routines for your inventory application. For application-specific copy members, it is a good idea to prefix member names with the identifier for the application, so all inventory copy members start with INV.

To make /COPY members really useful demands a little thought. Each copy member should include a header section that defines the function of the member, all input and output fields, and any dependent copy members that also must be included for compilation. /COPY members also must be thoroughly tested to make sure they work properly. However, if you do find a bug in one, you just edit the member and then use PDM's "find string" option to find and recompile all the affected programs.

/COPY lets you code faster, and maintain programs more easily, by focusing on the specifics of a program and storing reusable code in one central repository. Good candidates for copy members include commonly used data structures, field names, named constants, parameter lists, and low-level subroutines.

String Functions Test Program

Appendix B

Ensure that your libraries of reusable RPG routines work correctly by building interactive test programs.

When you build libraries of RPG functions, such as the string functions we presented in Chapters 16-19, you'll always want to test those functions thoroughly before you use them in production programs. When we build such libraries, we build test programs such as the one presented in this appendix. As you build your reusable libraries of RPG code, don't discount the value of building such testing programs. The time invested up front to build test programs like this pays off handsomely in the end.

To interactively test the 12 string functions presented in Chapters 16-19, use the RPG program TSTSTR this appendix provides. You'll find that experimenting with TSTSTR quickly adds to your understanding of the string functions and how they work. Compile instructions are included as comments in Figure B.1.

Figure B.1 TSTSTR RPG Program (Test String Functions)

```
... 1 ...+... 2 ...+... 3 ...+... 4 ...+... 5 ...+... 6 ...+... 7 ...+... 8

 *-------------------------------------------------------------------
 * TSTSTR - Test string functions
 *-------------------------------------------------------------------
 *
 * Function:
 *   Allows you to interactively test the twelve string functions
 *   presented in Chapters 16-19.
 *
 * To compile:
 *   1. Create the display file shown in Figure B.2 with CRTDSPF
 *
 *   2. Ensure that members:
 *        WSDS          WSCONS        STRDS         STDCONST
 *        STRCAT        STRCTR        STRFND        STRFNL
 *        STRLAJ        STRLEN        STRLWR        STRPAD
 *        STRRAJ        STRSUB        STRTRM        STRUPR
 *      are all available in a QRPGSRC source file. If you have
 *      these members in a source file with a different name,
 *      you'll need to qualify the /COPY references with the
```

Figure B.1 TSTSTR RPG Program (Test String Functions), continued

```
... 1 ...+... 2 ...+... 3 ...+... 4 ...+... 5 ...+... 6 ...+... 7 ...+... 8

     *       appropriate source file name.
     *
     *   3. Compile this program with CRTRPGPGM
     *----------------------------------------------------------------
     FTSTSTRD CF  E                     WORKSTN     KINFDS WSDS
     *
     I/COPY WSDS
     I/COPY WSCONS
     *
     I/COPY STRDS
     I/COPY STDCONST
     *
     C          *ON       DOWEQ*ON
     *
     C                    EXFMTTSTSTRR
     *
     C          WSKEY     IFEQ WSF03
     C          WSKEY     OREQ WSF12
     C                    LEAVE
     C                    ENDIF
     *
     C          SUITE     CASEQ'STRCAT'   STRCAT
     C          SUITE     CASEQ'STRCTR'   STRCTR
     C          SUITE     CASEQ'STRFND'   STRFND
     C          SUITE     CASEQ'STRFNL'   STRFNL
     C          SUITE     CASEQ'STRLAJ'   STRLAJ
     C          SUITE     CASEQ'STRLEN'   STRLEN
     C          SUITE     CASEQ'STRLWR'   STRLWR
     C          SUITE     CASEQ'STRPAD'   STRPAD
     C          SUITE     CASEQ'STRRAJ'   STRRAJ
     C          SUITE     CASEQ'STRSUB'   STRSUB
     C          SUITE     CASEQ'STRTRM'   STRTRM
     C          SUITE     CASEQ'STRUPR'   STRUPR
     C                    CAS             STRX
     C                    ENDCS
     *
     C                    ENDDO
     *
     C                    MOVE *ON        *INLR
     *
     C          STRX      BEGSR
     C                    MOVE *ON        STRERR
     C                    Z-ADD*HIVAL     STRP
     C                    ENDSR
     *
     C/COPY STRCAT
     C/COPY STRCTR
     C/COPY STRFND
     C/COPY STRFNL
     C/COPY STRLAJ
     C/COPY STRLEN
     C/COPY STRLWR
```

Figure B.1 TSTSTR RPG Program (Test String Functions), continued

```
... 1 ...+... 2 ...+... 3 ...+... 4 ...+... 5 ...+... 6 ...+... 7 ...+... 8


C/COPY STRPAD
C/COPY STRRAJ
C/COPY STRSUB
C/COPY STRTRM
C/COPY STRUPR
```

Figure B.2 TSTSTRD Display File DDS (Use with Figure B.1)

```
... 1 ...+... 2 ...+... 3 ...+... 4 ...+... 5 ...+... 6 ...+... 7 ...+... 8


     *------------------------------------------------------------------
     * TSTSTRD - Test string functions display file DDS
     *------------------------------------------------------------------
     A                                       DSPSIZ(24 80 *DS3)
     A                                       PRINT
     A                                       INDTXT(60 'SFLCLR')
     A                                       INDTXT(61 'SFLDSP')
     A                                       INDTXT(62 'SFLDSPCTL')
     A                                       INDTXT(63 'SFLEND')
     A                                       INDTXT(64 'SFLINZ')
     A                                       INDTXT(65 'SFLNXTCHG')
     A                                       INDTXT(66 'SFLBOF')
     A                                       INDTXT(70 'Record was changed')
     A                                       INDTXT(71 'Protect Fields')
     A                                       INDTXT(72 'Non-display Fields')
     A                                       INDTXT(73 'SFLFOLD')
     A                                       INDTXT(75 'Valid Command Key')
     A                                       INDTXT(76 'Error in Entry')
     A          R TSTSTRR
     A                                       TEXT('Test string functions')
     A                                       CA03
     A                                       CA12
     A                                       CHANGE(70)
     A                                       VLDCMDKEY(75)
     A                                       OVERLAY
     A                                       RTNDTA
     A                                       RTNCSRLOC(&FICRN &FICFN &FICPOS)
     A            FICRN        10A  H        TEXT('Cursor Record Name')
     A            FICFN        10A  H        TEXT('Cursor Field Name')
     A            FICPOS        4S OH        TEXT('Cursor Position')
     A                                    1  2'TSTSTR'
     A                                       COLOR(BLU)
     A                                    1 35'String Tests'
     A                                       DSPATR(HI)
     A                                    3  2'Type information, press Enter.'
     A                                       COLOR(BLU)
     A                                    5  2'SUITE :'
     A            SUITE         6A  B   5 10
     A                                    7  2'STR1  :'
     A            STR1        256A  B   8  1
     A                                   12  2'STR1LN:'
     A            STR1LN        3S OB  12 10
```

```
... 1 ...+... 2 ...+... 3 ...+... 4 ...+... 5 ...+... 6 ...+... 7 ...+... 8

A                                    12 22'STR1PS:'
A           STR1PS        3S 0B 12 30
A                                    12 42'STR1SZ:'
A           STR1SZ        3S 0B 12 50
A                                    14  2'STR2   :'
A           STR2         256A  B 15  1
A                                    19  2'STR2LN:'
A           STR2LN        3S 0B 19 10
A                                    19 22'STR2PS:'
A           STR2PS        3S 0B 19 30
A                                    19 42'STR2SZ:'
A           STR2SZ        3S 0B 19 50
A                                    21  2'STRERR:'
A           STRERR        1A  O 21 10
A                                    21 22'STRP   :'
A           STRP          3Y 0O 21 30EDTCDE(J)
A                                    23  2'F3=Exit'
A                                       COLOR(BLU)
A                                    23 13'F12=Cancel'
A                                       COLOR(BLU)
```

RPG Reference

Appendix C

Control Specifications

Position	Name	Entry
1-5	Sequence	Sequence identifier
6	Form type	H
7-14		
15	Debug	Blank, 1
16-17		
18	Currency symbol	Blank, currency symbol
19	Date format	Blank, M, D, Y
20	Date edit	Blank, any character
21	Decimal notation	Blank, I, J, D
22-25		
26	Alternate collating sequence	Blank, S
27-39		
40	Sign handling	Blank
41	Forms alignment	Blank, 1
42		
43	File translation	Blank, F
44-56		
55	Subprogram	Blank, S
57	Transparency check	Blank, 1
58-74		
75-80	Program identification	Program name

File Specifications
Main File Description Line Summary

Position	Name	Entry
1-5	Sequence	Sequence identifier
6	Form type	F
7-14	File name	File name
15	File type	I, O, U, C
16	File designation	Blank, P, S, R, T, F
17	End of file	Blank, E
18	Sequence	Blank, A, D
19	File format	F, E
20-23		
24-27	Record length	1-9999
28	Limits processing	Blank, L
29-30	Key length or record address field	Blank, 1-99
31	Record address type	Blank, A, P, K
32	File organization	Blank, I, T
33-34	Overflow indicators	Blank, OA-OG, OV, 01-99
35-38	Key field start location	Blank, 1-9999
39	Extension code	Blank, E, L
40-46	Device	PRINTER, DISK, WORKSTN, SPECIAL, SEQ
47-52		
53	Continuation lines	Blank, K
54-59	Routine name	Name of user routine
60-65		
66	File addition/unordered	Blank, A
67-70		
71-72	File condition	Blank, U1-U8, UC
73-74		
75-80	Comments	Optional

File Specifications
Continuation Line Summary

Position	Name	Entry
1-5	Sequence	Sequence identifier
6	Form type	F
7-18		
19-28		External name of record format
29-46		
47-52	Record number field for SFILE	Numeric field name
53	Continuation line	K
54-59, 60-67 [1]		
68-74		
75-80	Comments	Optional

[1] These positions are used together. Positions 54-59 specify the option, while positions 60-67 further explain the option.

File Specifications

Continuation Line Options Summary

Option (54-59)	Entry (60-67)	Explanation
COMIT		This file is specified for commitment control.
ID	Field name	Positions 60-65 contain the left-justified name of a 10-character alphanumeric field that requires no further definition. This field contains the name of the program device that supplied the record being processed in the file.
IGNORE		This option lets you ignore a record format from an externally described file.
IND	Indicator number	Indicators from 01 to the specified number are saved and restored for each device attached to a mixed- or multiple-device file.
INFDS	Data structure name	This entry lets you define and name a data structure to contain the exception/error information. The data structure name is entered in positions 60-65 and left-justified. If you specify INFDS for more than one file, each associated data structure must have a unique name.
INFSR	Subroutine name	The file exception/error subroutine named (left-justified) in positions 60-65 may receive control after file exceptions/errors. The subroutine name *PSSR indicates that the user-defined program exception/error subroutine is to receive control for errors on this file.
NUM	Maximum number of devices	The specified number must be greater than zero and right-justified in positions 60-65.

Continued on next page...

Continuation Line Options Summary, continued

Option (54-59)	Entry (60-67)	Explanation
PASS	*NOIND	Specify PASS *NOIND on the file-specification continuation line for a program-described WORKSTN file if you are taking responsibility for passing indicators on input and output.
PLIST	Parameter list name	This entry is valid only when the device specified in positions 40-46 of the main file description line is SPECIAL. Positions 60-65 give the left-justified name of the parameter list that is to be passed to the special routine.
PRTCTL	Data structure name	The dynamic printer-control option is being used. The data structure specified left-justified in positions 60-65 refers to the forms-control information and line-count value.
RECNO	Field name	This entry is optional for disk files to be processed by relative record number (RRN). A RECNO field must be specified for output files processed by RRN, output files referenced by a random WRITE calculation operation, or output files used with ADD on the output specifications.
RENAME	Record format name	This optional entry lets you rename record formats in an externally described file. Positions 19-28 of the continuation line specify the external name of the record format that is to be renamed. Positions 60-67 specify the left-justified name of the record as it is used in the program.
SAVDS	Data structure name	Positions 60-65 contain the left-justified name of the data structure that is saved and restored for each device.

Continued on next page...

Continuation Line Options Summary, continued

Option (54-59)	Entry (60-67)	Explanation
SFILE	Record format name	Positions 60-67 must specify, left-justified, the RPG name of the record format to be processed as a subfile. Positions 47-52 must specify the name of the relative record number field for this subfile.
SLN	Field name	Positions 60-65 contain the left-justified name of a start line number (SLN) field. The SLN field determines where a record format will be written to a display file.

Extension Specifications

Position	Name	Entry
1-5	Sequence	Sequence identifier
6	Form type	E
7-10		
11-18	From file name	Blank, record-address file name, array, or table file name
19-26	To file name	Blank, name of an input or update file containing data records, name of an output or combined file
27-32	Table or array name	Table or array name
33-35	Number of entries per record	Blank, 1-999
36-39	Number of entries per array or table	1-9999
40-42	Length of entry	1-256
43	Data format	Blank, P, B, L, R
44	Decimal positions	Blank, 0-9
45	Sequence	Blank, A, D
46-51	Table or array name (alternating format)	Table or array name (alternating format)
52-54	Length of entry	1-256
55	Data format	Blank, P, B, L, R
56	Decimal positions	Blank, 0-9
57	Sequence	Blank, A, D
58-80	Comments	Optional

Line Counter Specifications

Position	Name	Entry
1-5	Sequence	Sequence identifier
6	Form type	L
7-14	File name	File name
15-17	Number of lines per page	2-112
18-19	Form length	FL
20-22	Overflow line number	2-112
23-24	Overflow line	OL
25-74		
75-80	Comments	Optional

Input Specifications

Externally Described Files, Record Identification Entries

Position	Name	Entry
1-5	Sequence	Sequence identifier
6	Form type	I
7-14	Record name	Record format name
15-18		
19-20	Record-identifying indicators	Blank, 01-99, L1-L9, LR, H1-H9, U1-U8, RT
21-74		
75-80	Comments	Optional

Externally Described Files, Field Entries

Position	Name	Entry
1-5	Sequence	Sequence identifier
6	Form type	I
7-20		
21-30	External field name	Field name
31-52		
53-58	RPG field name	Field name
59-60	Control level	Blank, L1-L9
61-62	Match fields	Blank, M1-M9
63-64		
65-70	Field indicators	Blank, 01-99, H1-H9, U1-U8, RT
71-74		
75-80	Comments	Optional

Input Specifications

Program-Described Files, Record-Identification Entries

Position	Name	Entry
1-5	Sequence	Sequence identifier
6	Form type	I
7-14	File name	File name
14-16	Logical relationship	AND or OR
15-16	Sequence	Any two alphabetic characters, any two-digit number
17	Number	Blank, 1, N
18	Option	Blank, O
19-20	Record-identifying indicators	01-99, L1-L9, LR, H1-H9, U1-U8, RT, **
21-24, 28-31, 35-38	Position	Blank, 1-9999
25, 32, 39	Logical relationship	Blank, N
26, 33, 40	Code part	C, Z, D
27, 34, 41	Character	Any character
42-74		
75-80	Comments	Optional

Program-Described Files, Field-Description Entries

Position	Name	Entry
1-5	Sequence	Sequence identifier
6	Form type	I
7-42		
43	Data format	Blank, P, B, L, R
44-47	From	1-9999
48-51	To	1-9999
52	Decimal positions	Blank, 0-9
53-58	Field name	Symbolic name
59-60	Control level	Blank, L1-L9
61-62	Match fields	Blank, M1-M9
63-64	Field record relation	Blank, 01-99, L1-L9, MR, U1-U8, H1-H9, RT
65-70	Field indicators	Blank, 01-99, H1-H9, U1-U8, RT
71-74		
75-80	Comments	Optional

Input Specifications
Data-Structure Statement Specifications

Position	Name	Entry
1-5	Sequence	Sequence identifier
6	Form type	I
7-12	Data structure name	Blank, data structure name
13-16		
17	External description	Blank, E
18	Option	Blank, I, S, U
19-20	Record-identifying indicators	DS
21-30	External file name	External name of data structure
31-43		
44-47	Occurrences	Blank, 1-9999
48-51	Data structure length	Blank, 1-9999
52-74		
75-80	Comments	Optional

Data-Structure Subfield Specifications

Position	Name	Entry
1-5	Sequence	Sequence identifier
6	Form type	I
7-20		
8	Initialization option	Blank, I
9-20		
21-30	External field name	External name of subfield
21-42	Initialization value	Initial value
31-42		
43	Data format	Blank, P, B
44-47	From	1-9999
48-51	To	1-9999
44-51	Keywords	Keywords
52	Decimal positions	Blank, 0-9
53-58	Subfield name	Subfield name
59-74		
75-80	Comments	Optional

Input Specifications

Named Constant Specifications

Position	Name	Entry
1-5	Sequence	Sequence identifier
6	Form type	I
7-20		
21-42	Constant	Constant value
43	Data type	Blank, C
44-52		
53-58	Constant name	Name
59-74		
75-80	Comments	Optional

Calculation Specifications

Position	Name	Entry
1-5	Sequence	Sequence identifier
6	Form type	C
7-8	Control level	Blank, L0, L1-L9, LR, SR, AN, OR
9-17	Conditioning indicators	Blank, 01-99, KA-KN, KP-KY, L1-L9, LR, MR, H1-H9, RT, U1-U8, OA-OG, OV
18-27	Factor 1	Symbolic name or literal
28-32	Operation	Operation code
33-42	Factor 2	Symbolic name or literal
43-48	Result field	Field name
49-51	Field length	Blank, 1-15, 1-30, 1-256
52	Decimal positions	Blank, 0-9
53	Operation extender	Blank, P, H, N
54-59	Resulting indicators	Blank, 01-99, KA-KN, KP-KY, H1-H9, L1-L9, LR, OA-OG, OV, U1-U8, RT
60-80	Comments	Optional

Output Specifications

Externally Described Files, Record-Identification and Control Entries

Position	Name	Entry
1-5	Sequence	Sequence identifier
6	Form type	O
7-14	Record name	Record-format name
14-16	Logical relationship	AND or OR
15	Type	H, D, T, E
16	Release	R
16-18	Record addition field	ADD, DEL
16-22	Space/Skip, fetch overflow	Blank
23-31	Output indicators	Blank, 01-99, KA-KN, KP-KY, L1-L9, H1-H9, U1-U8, MR, LR, RT, 1P
32-37	EXCPT name	Record group name
38-74		
75-80	Comments	Optional

Externally Described Files, Field-Description and Control Entries

Position	Name	Entry
1-5	Sequence	Sequence identifier
6	Form type	O
7-22		
23-31	Field output indicators	See output indicators
32-37	Field name	Field name, *ALL
38		
39	Blank after	Blank, B
40-74		
75-80	Comments	Optional

Output Specifications

Program-Described Files, Record-Identification and Control Entries (Record Line)

Position	Name	Entry
1-5	Sequence	Sequence identifier
6	Form type	O
7-14	File name	File name
14-16	AND/OR	AND or OR
15	Type	H, D, T, E
16-18	ADD/DEL	ADD, DEL
16	Fetch overflow; Release	Blank, F, or R
17	Space before	Blank, 0, 1, 2, 3
18	Space after	Blank, 0, 1, 2, 3
19-20	Skip before	1-99, A0-A9, B0-B2
21-22	Skip after	1-99, A0-A9, B0-B2
23-31	Output indicators	Blank, 1-99, KA-KN, KP-KY, L1-L9, H1-H9,
32-37	EXCPT name	Record group name
38-74		
75-80	Comments	Optional

Program-Described Files, Field-Description and Control Entries (Field Line)

Position	Name	Entry
1-5	Sequence	Sequence identifier
6	Form type	O
7-22		
23-31	Field output indicators	See output indicators
32-37	Field name	Field name, PAGE, PAGE1-PAGE7,
38	Edit code	Blank, 1-4, 5-9, A-D, J-Q, X, Y, Z
39	Blank after	Blank, B
40-43	End position in output record	Blanks, +nnn, -nnn, nnnn, K1-K8
44	Data format	Blank, P, B, L, R, G
45-70	Constant or edit word	Constant or edit word, format name
71-74		
75-80	Comments	Optional

Operation Codes

- An empty column indicates that the field must be blank, or that there is no resulting indicator in that position.
- All underlined fields are required.
- Symbols:

(h)	Half adjust the result
(n)	Do not lock record on input if file is update
(p)	Pad the result with blanks
+	Plus
-	Minus
BL	Blank(s)
BN	Blank(s) then numeric
BOF	Beginning of file
EOF	End of file
EQ	Equal
ER	Error
FD	Found
HI	Greater than
IN	Indicator
LO	Less than
LR	Last record
NR	No record found
NU	Numeric
OF	Off
ON	On
Z	Zero
ZB	Zero or blank

Operation Code Specifications

Codes	Factor 1	Factor 2	Result Field	Resulting Indicators		
ACO	Device name	WORKSTN file			ER	
ADD (h)	Addend	Addend	Sum	+	-	Z
ANDxx	Comparand	Comparand				
BEGSR	Subroutine name					
BITOF		Bit numbers	Character field			
BITON		Bit numbers	Character field			
CABxx	Comparand	Comparand	Label	HI	LO	EQ
CALL		Program name	PLIST name		ER	LR
CASxx	Comparand	Comparand	Subroutine name	HI	LO	EQ
CAT (p)	Source string 1	Source string 2:number of blanks	Target string			
CHAIN (n)	Search argument	File name or record name	Data structure	NR	ER	
CHECK [2]	Comparator string	Base string:start	Leftmost position(s)		ER	FD
CHEKR [2]	Comparator string	Base string:start	Rightmost position(s)		ER	FD
CLEAR	*NOKEY	Structure or variable or record name				
CLOSE		File name			ER	
COMIT	Boundary				ER	
COMP [1]	Comparand	Comparand		HI	LO	EQ
DEBUG	Identifier	Output file	Debug information			
DEFN	*LIKE	Referenced field	Defined field			
DEFN	*NAMVAR or *EXTRN	External data area	Internal program area			
DELET	Search argument	File name		NR	ER	

Operation Code Specifications, continued

Codes	Factor 1	Factor 2	Result Field	Resulting Indicators		
DIV (h)	Dividend	Divisor	Quotient	+	-	Z
DO	Starting value	Limit value	Index value			
DOUxx	Comparand	Comparand				
DOWxx	Comparand	Comparand				
DSPLY	Message identifier	Output queue	Response		ER	
DUMP	Identifier					
ELSE						
END		Increment value				
ENDCS						
ENDDO		Increment value				
ENDIF						
ENDSL						
ENDSR	Label	Return point				
EXCPT		EXCPT name				
EXFMT		Record format name			ER	
EXSR		Subroutine name				
FEOD		File name			ER	
FORCE		File name				
FREE		Program name			ER	
GOTO		Label				
IFxx	Comparand	Comparand				
IN	*LOCK	Data area name			ER	
ITER						
KFLD			Key field			
KLIST	KLIST name					
LEAVE						

Continued on next page...

Operation Code Specifications, continued

Codes	Factor 1	Factor 2	Result Field	Resulting Indicators		
LOKUP[1]						
(array)	Search argument	Array name		HI	LO	EQ
(table)	Search argument	Table name	Table name	HI	LO	EQ
MHHZO		Source field	Target field			
MHLZO		Source field	Target field			
MLHZO		Source field	Target field			
MLLZO		Source field	Target field			
MOVE (p)		Source field	Target field	+	-	ZB
MOVEA (p)		Source	Target	+	-	ZB
MOVEL (p)		Source field	Target field	+	-	ZB
MULT (h)	Multiplicand	Multiplier	Product	+	-	Z
MVR			Remainder	+	-	Z
NEXT	Program device	File name			ER	
OCUR	Occurrence value	Data structure	Occurrence value		ER	
OPEN		File name			ER	
ORxx	Comparand	Comparand				
OTHER						
OUT	*LOCK	Data area name			ER	
PARM	Target field	Source field	Parameter			
PLIST	PLIST name					
POST [3]	Program device	File name or record name	INFDS name		ER	
READ (n)		File name or record name	Data structure		ER	EOF
READC		Record name			ER	EOF
READE (n)	Search argument	File name or record name	Data structure		ER	EOF

Continued on next page...

Operation Code Specifications, continued

Codes	Factor 1	Factor 2	Result Field	Resulting Indicators		
READP (n)		File name or record name	Data structure		ER	BOF
REDPE (n)	Search argument	File name or record name	Data structure		ER	BOF
REL	Program device	File name			ER	
RESET	*NOKEY	Structure or variable or record name			ER	
RETRN						
ROLBK					ER	
SCAN [2]	Comparator string:length	Base string:start	Leftmost position(s)		ER	FD
SELEC						
SETGT	Search argument	File name or record name		NR	ER	
SETLL	Search argument	File name or record name		NR	ER	EQ
SETOF [1]				OF	OF	OF
SETON [1]				ON	ON	ON
SHTDN				ON		
SORTA		Array name				
SQRT (h)		Value	Root			
SUB (h)	Minuend	Subtrahend	Difference	+	-	Z
SUBST (p)	Length to extract	Base string:unit	Target string		ER	
TAG	Label					
TESTB [1]		Bit numbers	Character field	OF	ON	EQ
TESTN [1]			Character field	NU	BN	BL
TESTZ [1]			Character field			
TIME			Numeric field			
UNLCK		Data area or file name			ER	

Continued on next page...

Operation Code Specifications, continued

Codes	Factor 1	Factor 2	Result Field	Resulting Indicators		
UPDAT		File name or record name	Data structure		ER	
WHxx	Comparand	Comparand				
WRITE		File name or record name	Data structure		ER	EOF
XFOOT (h)		Array name	Sum	+	-	Z
XLATE (p)	From:To	String:start	Target string		ER	FD
Z-ADD (h)		Addend	Sum	+	-	Z
Z-SUB (h)		Subtrahend	Difference	+	-	Z

[1] At least one resulting indicator is required.

[2] A found indicator is required if the result field is not specified.

[3] You must specify Factor 2 or the result field. You may specify both.

Editing Numeric Fields

Edit Code	Commas	Decimal Point	Sign for Negative Balance	O or Blanks	I	J
1	Yes	Yes	No sign	.00 or 0	,00 or 0	0,00 or 0
2	Yes	Yes	No sign	Blanks	Blanks	Blanks
3		Yes	No sign	.00 or 0	,00 or 0	0,00 or 0
4		Yes	No sign	Blanks	Blanks	Blanks
5-9	User-defined					
A	Yes	Yes	CR	.00 or 0	,00 or 0	0,00 or 0
B	Yes	Yes	CR	Blanks	Blanks	Blanks
C		Yes	CR	.00 or 0	,00 or 0	0,00 or 0
D		Yes	CR	Blanks	Blanks	Blanks
J	Yes	Yes	- (minus)	.00 or 0	,00 or 0	0,00 or 0
K	Yes	Yes	- (minus)	Blanks	Blanks	Blanks
L		Yes	- (minus)	.00 or 0	,00 or 0	0,00 or 0
M		Yes	- (minus)	Blanks	Blanks	Blanks
N	Yes	Yes	- (floating minus)	.00 or 0	,00 or 0	0,00 or 0
O	Yes	Yes	- (floating minus)	Blanks	Blanks	Blanks
P		Yes	- (floating minus)	.00 or 0	,00 or 0	0,00 or 0
Q		Yes	- (floating minus)	Blanks	Blanks	Blanks
X [1]						
Y [2]						
Z [3]						

[1] The X edit code ensures a plus sign for positive values.

[2] The Y edit code is normally used to edit a date field with 3 to 9 digits. It suppresses the leftmost zeros of date fields, up to but not including the digit preceding the first separator. The Y edit code also inserts slashes (/) between the month, day, and year according to the following pattern:

```
nn/n
nn/nn
nn/nn/n
nn/nn/nn
nnn/nn/nn
nn/nn/nnnn      Format used with M, D, or blank in position 19
nnn/nn/nnnn     Format used with M, D, or blank in position 19
nnnn/nn/nn      Format used with Y in position 19
nnnnn/nn/nn     Format used with Y in position 19
```

[3] The Z edit code removes the sign (plus or minus) from a numeric field and suppresses leading zeros of a numeric field.

Note: All entries are zero-suppressed.

RPG Special Words

The following RPG reserved words have special functions in a program:

- UDATE, UDAY, UMONTH, UYEAR, *DATE, *DAY, *MONTH, and *YEAR let you access the system date, or a portion of it, for program use.
- PAGE, PAGE1-PAGE7 can be used for numbering the pages of a report, for record-sequence numbering, or for sequentially numbering output fields.
- Figurative constants (*BLANK/*BLANKS, *ZERO/*ZEROS, *HIVAL, *LOVAL, *ON/*OFF, *ALLX'x1..', and *ALL'X..') are implied literals that allow specifications without referring to length.
- *IN and *Inxx let indicators be referred to as data.
- The following reserved words define symbolic locations in the file information data structure and the program status data structure: *FILE, *OPCODE, *PARMS, *PROGRAM, *RECORD, *ROUTINE, and *STATUS.
- The following reserved words provide symbolic labels for the ENDSR operation for the file and program exception/error subroutines or for the file information data structure:

*CANCL	Cancel the program
*DETC	Detail calculations
*DETL	Detail lines
*GETIN	Get input record
*INIT	Program initialization
*OFL	Overflow lines
*TERM	Program ending
*TOTC	Total calculations
*TOTL	Total lines

- The following special words are used with operation codes: *DEFN, *ENTRY, *INZSR, *LDA, *LIKE, *LOCK, *NAMVAR, *OFF, *ON, *PDA, and *PSSR.
- The following special words are used with translation: *EQUATE and *FILE.
- *PLACE allows repetitive placement of fields in an output record.
- *ALL lets all fields defined for an externally described file be written on output.

RPG Restrictions

Function	Restriction
AN/OR lines (positions 7 and 8 of calculation specifications)	Maximum of 7 per operation
Arrays	Maximum of 200 per program
Array input record length for compile time	Maximum length is 80
Character field length	Maximum length is 256
Control fields (positions 59 and 60 of input specifications) length	Maximum length is 256
Data structure length	Maximum of 9999
Data structure occurrences	Maximum of 9999 per data structure
Edit word	Maximum length of 24 for literals or 115 for named constants
Elements in an array/table (positions 36-39 of extension specifications)	Maximum of 9999 per array/table
File	Maximum of 50 per program
Levels of nesting in structured groups	Maximum of 100
Look-ahead	Can be specified only once for a file; can be specified only for primary and secondary files
Named constant	Maximum length of 256 for character named constant, 512 for hexadecimal named constant, and 30 digits with 9 decimal positions for numeric named constant
Numeric field length	Maximum 30 digits, 9 decimal places
Overflow indicator	Only 1 unique overflow indicator can be specified per printer file
Parameters	Maximum of 255
Primary file (P in position 16 of file specifications)	Maximum of 1 per program
Printer file (PRINTER in positions 40-46 of file specifications)	Maximum of 8 per program
Printing lines per page	Maximum of 112; minimum of 2
Program status data structure	Only 1 allowed per program

Continued on next page...

RPG Restrictions, continued

Function	Restriction
Record address file (R in position 16 of file specifications)	Only 1 allowed per program
Record length for program-described file (positions 24-27 of file specifications)	Maximum length is 9999 [1]
Subroutines	Maximum of 254 per program
Tables	Maximum of 200 per program
Table input record length for compile time	Maximum length is 80

[1] Any device record size restraints override this value.

Error Handling
File Error Codes
Normal Conditions

Codes	Meaning
00000	No exception/error occurred.
00002	Function key used to end display.
00011	End of file on a read (input).
00012	No record found on a CHAIN, SETGT, SETLL operation.
00013	Subfile is full on a write operation.

Exception/Error Conditions

Codes	Meaning
01011	Undefined record type (input record does not match record-identifying indicator).
01021	Tried to write a record that already exists (file being used has unique keys and key is duplicate, or attempted to use duplicate relative record number to a subfile).
01031	Match field out of sequence.
01041	Array/table load sequence error.
01051	Excess entries in array/table file.
01071	Numeric sequence error.
01121	No indicator on the DDS keyword for Print key.
01122	No indicator on the DDS keyword for Roll up key.
01123	No indicator on the DDS keyword for Roll down key.
01124	No indicator on the DDS keyword for Clear key.
01125	No indicator on the DDS keyword for Help key.
01126	No indicator on the DDS keyword for Home key.
01201	Record mismatch detected on input.
01211	I/O operation to a closed file.
01215	OPEN issued to a file already open.
01216	Error on an implicit OPEN/CLOSE operation.

Continued on next page...

Exception/Error Conditions, continued

Codes	Meaning
01217	Error on an explicit OPEN/CLOSE operation.
01218	Record already locked.
01221	Update operation attempted without a prior read.
01231	Error on SPECIAL file.
01235	Error in PRTCTL space or skip entries.
01241	Record number not found. (Record number specified in record address file is not present in file being processed.)
01251	Permanent I/O error occurred.
01255	Session or device error occurred. Recovery may be possible.
01261	Attempt to exceed maximum number of acquired devices.
01281	Operation to unacquired device.
01282	Job ending with controlled option.
01285	Attempt to acquire a device already acquired.
01286	Attempt to open shared file with SAVDS or IND options.
01287	Response to indicators overlap IND indicators.
01299	Other I/O error detected.
01331	Wait time exceeded for READ from WORKSTN file.

Error Handling

Program Status Codes

Normal Conditions

Codes	Meaning
00000	No exception/error occurred.
00001	Called program returned with indicator LR on.

Exception/Error Conditions

Codes	Meaning
00100	Value out of range for string operation.
00101	Negative square root.
00102	Divide by zero.
00121	Invalid array index.
00122	OCUR outside range.
00123	RESET attempted during initialization subroutine.
00202	Called program failed; halt indicator (H1-H9) not on.
00211	Program specified on CALL or FREE not found.
00221	Called program tried to use a parameter not passed to it.
00231	Called program returned with halt indicator on.
00232	Halt indicator on in this program.
00233	Halt indicator on when RETRN operation run.
00299	RPG formatted dump failed.
00333	Error on DSPLY operation.
00401	Data area specified on IN or OUT not found.
00402	*PDA not valid for non-prestart job.
00411	Data area types or lengths do not match.
00412	Data area not locked for output.
00413	Error on IN or OUT operation.
00414	User not authorized to use data area.
00415	User not authorized to change data area.

Continued on next page...

Exception/Error Conditions, continued

Codes	Meaning
00421	Error on UNLCK operation.
00431	Data area previously locked by another program.
00432	Data area locked by program in the same process.
00907	Decimal data error (invalid digit or sign).
00970	The level numbers of the generating compiler and the runtime subroutines do not match.
09998	Internal failure in RPG compiler or in runtime subroutines.
09999	Program exception in system routine.

Note: For more detailed reference information, refer to IBM's *RPG/400 Reference* (SC09-1817).